The Metaphysical Wings of Man and Woman

Understanding our Being

Nicole Schomberg

Mazo Publishers

**The Metaphysical Wings of Man and Woman:
Understanding our Being**

ISBN 978-1-956381-672

Copyright © 2024 Nicole Schomberg

Contact the Author
nicoleschomberg@gmail.com

Mazo Publishers
Website: www.mazopublishers.com
Email: mazopublishers@gmail.com

Cover Image by Alona Dorit

54321
All rights reserved.
No part of this publication may be translated, reproduced, stored in a retrieval system, or transmitted in any form or by any means, electronic, mechanical, photocopying, recording or otherwise, without prior permission in writing.

This book is dedicated to

my late mother Esther,

daughter of Sima'h & Fortunée

Contents

	Introduction	7
Chapter I	In the Beginning	9
Chapter II	Destruction and Creation	13
Chapter III	The Meaning of Linguistics of Life	21
Chapter IV	The Interrelation Between Language and Body Language	23
Chapter V	The Projection of Man	31
Chapter VI	The Search for the Wing	35
Chapter VII	Some Basic Instruments of the Wings	41
Chapter VIII	Double Standards	47
Chapter IX	Removing the Outer Shell of Man	55
Chapter X	The Inner Shell of Man	63
Chapter XI	The Spirit of Man	73
Chapter XII	The Shape of Woman	81
Chapter XIII	The Instrument of Thought and Speech	85
Chapter XIV	Numbers, Letters and Figures	93
Chapter XV	Classification	103
Chapter XVI	Politics	111
Chapter XVII	Relationships	117
Chapter XVIII	Shape, Movement and Wings	129
Chapter XIX	The Psychology of the Triangular Philosophy	135
Chapter XX	The Spiritual and Physical Linkage	141

Introduction

Man and woman, whether they are conscious of the fact, live by philosophy. It governs their way of life, how they think and how they conduct themselves. But it would be true to say that most people in the hurly burly of modern living do not recognize this fact and therefore, to their disadvantage lack an understanding of themselves and the environment in which they live.

The Metaphysical Wings of Man and Woman has been written with one objective in mind and that is to obtain unity of the linguistics of life in its broader sense and to give the initiated and the uninitiated insights into three-dimensional thinking rather than in an automatic two-dimensional manner, where the beauty of physical and spiritual life is hidden under a shroud.

It would be true to say that what a man sees and how he thinks not only embraces his whole being, enough to reach the output of every condition and circumstance in his life.

The philosophy expressed here is based on the triangular linguistics of life, including body language and focuses on the research linking science to meaningful relationships between movement and shape and the imaginary wings of Man so that the reader may be encouraged outthink three dimensionally and in geometrical shapes when doing such mundane tasks as washing in the morning, eating, talking, thinking and outlearn how to observe himself in his own environment instead of giving himself up entirely to the whirlwind of modern day fragmented existence.

Above all this is an appeal to the Spirit of Man in an attempt to channel and develop itself in spite of the materialistic approach of the consumer society.

A newly-wed couple in honeymoon... Here he comes with his angle and here she comes with her triangle. He waits for her to direct him with her remote control triangular device. He is going to stick his angle onto the triangle he chose for life and which will direct him either for the best or for the worst.

Chapter I
In the Beginning

In the beginning there existed in the world a pre-void in so far as the word was concerned. A movement was unformed and there was no regulated life in the body. In the Bible it is referred to as the void of Darkness. Then came the Light, which regulated movements of the body through instinct. The voice was still in the darkness without shape or form and was a silent part of the body.

On the second stage of creation as described in the Bible the waters were divided. In so far as the body was concerned, the division occurred between body language and the mouth from which came out sound.

In the third stage the water was put in one part of the world to allow the Earth to rise from the waters. In so far as the body was concerned, everything was put into one place similarly to the waters allowing articulated and controlled sound to rise out of the substance of man, in the same way as the Earth rose out of the waters.

On the fourth stage the sun appeared, as did the moon. The sun regulating the day and the moon regulating the night. In the same way body language came out of the darkness into the light, as did the sun. The mouth remained in darkness and represented the moon.

During the fifth stage there appeared life in the water and on the Earth and the first commandment in the Bible was to be fruitful and multiply. In the same way, language in its spoken and visual form started to take shape and there is nothing that can multiply more fruitfully than language.

In the sixth stage each creature developed its own kind and man and woman were to dominate them all. There was food for every living creature and the commandment remained unchanged.

Then, at this stage speech took over from body language until the seventh stage, which was the stage of rest. The Semitic languages have retained much of the various stages of the creation as described above. Three of their main features emphasize this. First of all they contain guttural and laryngeal letters having unique sounds deeply connected with the concept of life. Secondly, the construction of almost all verbs and nouns comes from the three-letter root and thirdly the meaning depends upon the former pattern of words viewed in the overall context. Guttural sound is found in the word '**hai**' which means 'life' in Hebrew and Arabic. The '**h**' comes from the back of the throat, from the root of breath rather than from the front of the mouth. In the course of time all that has been retained of the original stages of speech is the vowel. Non-Semitic languages do not hold a three-letter root and in this way they seem to have lost the three-dimensional world of the heaven, earth and sea.

In Hebrew, the words 'writer', 'story', 'tell' and 'library' for instance are constructed from the same three root letters. In non-Semitic languages the links have been broken. All that remains is that the word can still be understood from its general context as a particular star can be recognized within the general context of the cosmos.

All languages still retain a common denominator e.g. the '**Yod**' made out of two sounds, hinging all the other sounds together in order to reach articulated speech. The consonants are nothing without the general contextual life surrounding them. They are like the bones, which are nothing without the general context of all body life. At death, they just crumble, as would the consonants without vowels, air and the whole construction of the body.

There are many languages, which in spite of their diversity come from the same breath and are as universal as body language. The Mother tongue heard at birth is the body language, which has the most profound effect and cannot be wiped out of the tissular memory, as the water cannot be entirely removed from the Earth. Body language and speech link into one register of language. Both link into one for all human activity, from the planting of seeds to the shaking of hands, up to legal or scientific speech.

There are many levels of language. The one that most men and women refer to when language is mentioned refers to communication between people by means of their vocal chords. What rarely occurs is that in trying to understand and analyze this kind of language, no attempt is made to analyze life itself.

From mere observation of the language described above, it has clearly become apparent that a grain of wheat is a grain of life that can reappear countless times if planted under the right conditions. In this regard, it seems that the linguistic grain of life can be linked to the soft "**ye** sound", or "**yod**" which appears as a diphthong whatever its various shapes may be in any of the existing human languages. It is from this primitive sound that humans are able to communicate between themselves and that human language has been able to develop as it has done. This sound is a directing thread which links all the various human languages serving as an embryo, in the same way as the most infinitesimal particle of life has served as the basic element in the theory of evolution of the species defined by Darwin. Composed out of two sounds linked together, thus sound follows the breathing pattern of inspiration and expiration of air by which we live. Being made out of two elements, it follows the pattern four two basic wings, which allow us to fly. There is still a flight involved at this stage of communication. The rest of the sounds are only for convenience, our third and fourth wing being all directed by the two antennae, which bring to our life another dimension. As far as sounds are concerned, there is the sound of the top of the pops that of nursery sounds, that of national anthems, that of religious chanting and hymns, and so on.

The top of the pops sound appeals to some through its pulsations, but is generally short lived like a soap bubble that lasts a short while then disappears to allow for more and more bubbles which come and form an endless stream leaving nothing in their wake. It is a most interesting fact that nursery songs outlive pop songs in spite of the fact, and perhaps thanks to the fact that they lacked the mass media support that we now have. The reason is that they give one important message – the message of survival. Let's take for example the nursery rhyme *Humpty Dumpy*.

> *Humpty Dumpy sat on a wall*
> *Humpty Dumpy had a great fall*
> *All the King's horses and*
> *All the King's men*
> *Could not put Humpty Dumpy*
> *Together again.*

As Humpty Dumpty sat precariously on a wall so we stand on the edge of a precipice. Should we fall like Humpty Dumpy then all the elements four structures would disintegrate, similar to the large egg represented by Humpty Dumpty. The shell would fragment, the yoke would break and the white would drain away. No power could then reunite the three dimensions of our being.

Chapter II
Destruction and Creation

There appears to be a built-in creative and destructive impulse within the structure of man. This impulse commences with a baby who rejects some item of food given by his or her mother. This generally occurs when the baby has been removed from the natural way of feeding i.e., the breast. A baby does not know the difference between these two movements; the drawing line between his movements still being very frail and not clearly defined.

Destruction basically falls into two categories, the physical destruction of matter and the attempted destruction of the soul.

Let us first consider physical destruction. It starts with the baby's rejection of food and this early rejection becomes destructive as the baby develops into a child who is prone to example. The child sees his or her parents in the various acts of physical destruction during his daily life, for instance the swatting of a fly, the crushing underfoot of an insect. In the kitchen we drop a cup or smash a glass, we smash an egg or open and throw away an empty tin of food. There is no differentiation in all these acts. As the parents explain the different things, the child learns that the mother is upset to have broken the glass or cup, but has broken the shell of the egg purposely. With the further development of the child, he will see how far he will affect his parents by tearing a newspaper, by breaking a piece of furniture in order to see how far he can influence his parents and obtain attention through destruction.

This is destruction in its simplest form. But one cannot even begin to analyze destruction from a philosophical point of view until it misunderstood what part destruction plays in creation and how it is vitally linked to Nature. It would seem that you couldn't have creation without destruction or destruction without creation. Also, from destruction comes transformation so that the full circle or cycle is complete. In the beginning, there is creation or destruction then, from this stems life; following life stems the cloak of death, which can either be viewed as destruction or creation leading to transformation. We can see this through observing Nature, particularly a tree that in the spring expands and transforms into a mass of moist green foliage and takes the essence of life throughout the summer. In the autumn the leaves change color and for a time display glorious hues of red, brown, etc. Then the leaves fall touch the ground, crumble and die. The tree remains alive and within it the seed of the next generation of foliage exists. The leaves in the daytime usually move up towards the light and at night turn downwards. Here you have creation and destruction leading to transformation as the full circle is completed from spring to winter.

A further example is the planting of grains of wheat. On the surface the seed is annihilated and negated, but when ideal conditions occur through fertile earth, water and light, it multiplies in its thousands. The shape of the wheat grain is split into two and all gathered in one shell. From its parted shape we can see two elements in one structure too that can also be destruction and creation, water and fire, light and darkness, the soul and the body all separated by a very thin line, still linked undergone. There is no padding in the overall shape of the seed, the sign being in front of our eyes. There is only a little nothing between two poles, and creation and destruction are part of numerous poles. The seed was annihilated, yet gave life. It seems that the more a matter seems to be destroyed, the more it will transform itself and reappear in greater glory.

Scientists when analyzing the formation of the world do not deny that the original gigantic destruction led to creation and gave birth to the first living cells. For the non-scientific approach, G-d created mankind in his image. In this respect is man able to destroy through a desire to create? Or is he destroying for the sheer pleasure of destruction?

Some psychologists believe that children at a certain stage of infancy cannot part with their own toys, because they are one and giving them away would be like giving a part of themselves, so that another child wishing to possess the object would provoke a fight and destruction of the object might occur in this case; destroying the object would be a form of possessing differently. This example may explain why man sometimes destroys objects, matter, worlds, in order to possess them in a different way what he cannot acquire and by acquiring it this way, he would acquire part of the people who created this object, matter, worlds etc. But can this analysis follow when applied to the destruction of another man. Each man is a cosmos to himself and the human brain being larger than the universe. Laws that regulate the statutes of men divided the slaughtering of man either by will of by accident and conceived minute legal statutes which branched off to give shape to criminology.

We shall concentrate on the conscious killing of man. How can there be creation through the killing of a man? Although this miracle seems impossible, it was once achieved in human history according to biblical data during the sacrifice of Isaac when Abraham did not hesitate to negate his generation in order to please G-d, by showing him infinite trust. By his gesture Abraham converted human death into a new lease of life. He transformed animal man into human man and the Jewish year starts from this act, which transformed evil into good and converted death for sacrificial purposes into life.

In this day and age, if a man was to display similar trust towards his Maker, he would be charged with attempted murder of the child and sent either to prison or to a psychiatric hospital. People that might have displayed such a trust and direct communication with their Maker would have been labeled as sorcerers and burnt or nailed to a cross or destroyed in other ways when sophisticated prisons and asylums were not conceived by a Welfare State. How far then can one "destroy" in order to create? It seems that once it is no more possible to convert evil into good, destruction will not lead to creation. It will perhaps be transformed in the long run into a different form of creation, but basically it appears as a negative destruction.

The instruments of destruction such as armaments of all size and description are the product of man's creativeness to kill i.e., destroy. Here again you have creativeness for destruction and the thin dividing line is aptly displayed. The weapons are filling a void where linguistic arguments have failed to be constructive. The ultimate is, of course, nuclear power, which in effect is filling a void by fear, when it appears that amicable argument between two political ideologies has failed. Fear has always been inherent to man's structure. The nuclear argument gives fear shape that can be molded according to the whims of the political leaders. It is a double-bladed instrument but, unlike the double-bladed seed of wheat, it seems to produce more negation than expansion. Fear can also conceal hate, in that the dividing line between love and hate is similar to that which exists between absorption and rejection, creation and destruction. To analyze the causes is almost impossible as they are so varied and numerous, but in humans it is generally caused by loss of oneness.

Every man has his own axis from which he derives his impulse and his energies through movement, which is the key of life and sometimes due to the unequal movement of the position of the axis, this source of energy is slightly deviated. Indifference occurs mainly when the axes are miles apart, which leads to destruction of a relationship where links are cut one by one.

However, in our day and age with the making of instruments of various sorts, the consumer society is creating an even worse instrument by advertising and publicity, whose sole purpose is to direct man towards other axes, poles and made easy exits which are portrayed as being the keys of happiness. Publicity and advertising are also backed by another danger, that of distraction, which has a related purpose, numbing man's vital impulse in that he is led to passively listen to well-designed political discussions, films, entertainers etc. until his purpose descends into the realm of forgetfulness. These gestures correspond to a current of water let loose without any holding power and without a force of will. Infants enter the world by clenching their fists and men die by opening their hands. This observation of one feature of life shows how far our purpose which is to "take" in order to live, has deviated as we grow to maturity when we give up more and more of our soul for the sake of physical pleasure and moral entertainment. The soul is that part of Man which can never be destroyed and which will always survive him in spite of all instruments of destruction, whether the destruction came from love or from hate. Nevertheless, it seems that the soul can empty itself from within through the power of willed internal destruction until there is not a drop of fire left since the soul appears as being the fire of the spirit. Man was given dominion over water and earth and currently appears to have given up dominion over the fire. Yet, he seems to want to dominate fire by using weapons and instruments of fire, as if it was possible to fulfill one's pulsation of life through weapons that destroy for the sake of destruction when body language has failed, because it was never understood. It is also another easy way out to think that, because G-d might have final dominion over fire, we should try either to destroy human beings through fire or give up the kindling part of our being that is the soul.

In the same way as Nature revives cycles of life and

destruction, aided man will perhaps live again through the same cycle. But this does not give any man the right to kill.

If one believes in the shape of the general law of nature, let us remember the example of the grain of wheat which lost its shape, whose structure became only a ghost, which nevertheless multiplied into many other fully structured shapes after its kind, which can be consumed four the benefit of all. If one could give a similar shape to creative destruction, which would have the potential source of energy to be fruitful and multiply, then there can be no void. Some call it reincarnation, others, resurrection.

This possibility of another kind of life beyond the one we experience is not an argument sufficient enough to give up earthly life in order to find a better fulfillment in the other world. G-d must have enough angels to serve Him and no doubt would appreciate earthly messengers who would take the time to read the signs He has given to us very visibly together with the principle of life stated in the Bible, the most read and misread book in the world taken for granted and wrongly consumed as a slice of orange, a peanut, a cigarette puff or a melody.

In a way it seems evident that evil can be transformed into good from the earth and from human beings, having understood themselves in order to achieve oneness and preferring to be cured by energetic medicine such as acupuncture, osteopathy etc. which use pain as a vital force which can create balance in the overall body, rather than numb the pain regardless of its source or calling sorcerers for another passive approach.

If there is a limitless source of energy, it is to be found within man rather than outside him and every human individual will never run short of it, if he only takes the time to carefully treasure it by not letting it stagnate. The more baby sucks mother's milk the more milk appears; once the suckling stops the milk stops. The control of this energy force lies in the knowledge and wisdom of when to use it and when to refrain from using it. This is a situation in which man cannot just take, but only take sufficiently so that the energy force can be recharged. In this respect more attention should be given to body language because this is the only language that does not fake and allows the core of man to express itself following its rhythmic productive movement and converting the deathlike into a lifeline.

Chapter III
THE MEANING OF LINGUISTICS OF LIFE

In this latter part of the twentieth century when most people are totally immersed in the materialistic aspect of our consumer society, the true meaning of life and even its purpose has almost disappeared from the minds of modern man and woman. We seem to be no longer concerned or even recognize the natural beauty of the world around us, which constitutes the third dimension and in religion is known as the soul or spiritual plane.

For the purpose of this book, it is necessary to define the two planes of life, the spiritual or soul plane and the material plane. In fact, these planes are interrelated and it would appear that man has two souls, one that desires to get close to G-d and the other that wants to move away from G-d.

The linguistics of life is the language of life. It is the language that surrounds us every moment of every day and gives us the impulse to live. It is based on the whole cosmos and is within man's inner self. It is far more than instinct. It is both physical and spiritual and produces the very life force of living entities.

In the beginning man fought nature and, therefore, did not recognize even the existence of the Language of Life. Then, when he vaguely became aware of its existence, he was unable to interpret it due to the narrow confines imposed by religious dogma and social convention. In modern times, these constraints have largely been removed, but another barrier to awareness has come into being by the over-emphasis of scientific study through the electron microscope. This has created over-concentration on the narrow analysis of the infinitesimal and has completely ignored the overall shapes and design of the basic structure of life.

It is seen in the flight of a bird, in a rose petal that falls to the ground in a strong summer breeze. It is seen in the triangle of a wing, the minute law of gravity and in the beak of a bird that pecks food from the ground with his or her companion. It is seen in the inverse movement of the two triangles of its beak and in its relationship one with the other. It is seen in the nerve pattern of a leaf and is inscribed in the palm of our hand and at the tip of our tongue. At night we dream of it because the constraints of living are removed. In the daytime our awareness is blurred, but the cycle of forgetfulness cannot be eternal, because our inner consciousness pecks at the linguistic truth from day to day, night to night thus inducing into us the vital breath of awareness of the philosophy of shapes and figures. Also, it is in the very basis of our ability to communicate between people and nations; in other words the importance to recognize the structure of language and its shape and purpose in the overall design of the cosmos. Further, it is necessary to have a true knowledge of figures and what they represent so that a unified theory of the triangle of life that exists outside of the mechanical use of the electron microscope and computer, can be understood. The triangle being, shapes, figures and philosophy.

To really understand what to many is a mystery, it will be necessary to define language, the analysis of shapes and the principle of numbers. In this way we will leave behind the restrictions of darkness in one-dimensional thinking and enter other dimensions, thereby reaching a wider understanding of ourselves and the cosmos of which we are part.

Chapter IV
THE INTERRELATION BETWEEN LANGUAGE AND BODY LANGUAGE

In every language there are consonants and vowels that have specific sound and shape. The consonants are the closure of the shape and the vowels are the shape still open. The two sounds and shapes are necessary; otherwise the language would be a jumble of indefinable sound without shape or purpose. However, one cannot articulate by the sole use of consonants, but we can articulate by solely using vowels. The vocalic sound appears to be the vital basic sound in the same way, as open shapes appear as necessary, because they allow communication.

In some languages the vowels are written on each side of the consonants, for example: Orange. In other languages such as Arabic and Hebrew most vowels have to be guessed. They are the soul of the consonant and live within it without being seen. Only the consonant appears so that the word has to be known in advance and can only be brought into its shape up inserting in the mind the "missing vowels". Therefore, it is necessary to try and understand the body of each letter, which make up the word before life can be instilled into it.

The life of the word is given in two ways, either by understanding its meaning in relationship to other words to which it is linked or by pronouncing it. In this latter way it has a different life and does not germinate any more in the spirit of the individual, but is released into the cosmos. If the sound elaborates matter, the concept of the sound also produces it as thought.

An interesting factor regarding this concerns a mother with a fetus in her womb. When she talks, she creates vibrations, which enter the fetus and thus she is shaping, already at this early stage, the basic physical and spiritual structure of the embryo.

In our everyday life and due to the automatic and common usage of words, the shape and sound of words, as well as the awareness of life they represent, is often lost to us. The reason for this is that our hearing and our visual senses are too familiar so that they are shrouded and their message is lost.

Let us consider two vowels linked together which produces the diphthong. In France when one suffers sudden pain, it is not unusual to exclaim "Aye!" The English express pain by "Ouch!" Apart from a few other sounds the French language is not based on the diphthong. This isn't the case with English and American, which are languages where diphthongs are commonly used and form the body and texture of the sound of these languages; it is not by chance that English and American have developed internationally as against other languages. Political and economic supremacy is not a convincing explanation, but the psychology of linguistics is of paramount importance in the development and status with which these languages have obtained.

The diphthong, e.g., two vowels linked together gives two open shapes also linked together, which will contract to give maximum life and birth to that part of life, which is hidden. From all sounds it appears that the Hebrew sound "yod" is the primary sound. It is also a basic diphthong. In the Hebrew alphabet where each letter corresponds to a number, the "yod" is assimilated to the number 10. We have ten fingers in our hands, five fingers in each hand and five muscular chains that regulate our life. Therefore, there is no mathematical psychology or minutely linguistic regulated order of the sound and shape of the cosmos. All is there for purpose and with awareness comes the knowledge that the signs and indications are to enlighten man to his spiritual and physical consciousness.

A "tick" or check mark which resembles the symbol used for the correct answer to a question could represent the sound of the diphthong in which the two vowels have a life-giving cut. This symbol also represents the flight of a bird in the distance. It is an open-ended triangle, which could represent the limitlessness of the cosmos and also its perfection. Although I suggest this sign could represent the diphthong, in fact in linguistics strangely enough there is no sign to present it. There is only a listing of possible diphthongs. It could be an "a" followed by and "i" or an "i" followed by an "a" or an "o" followed by an "i" etc. etc.

The more difficult the concept is to express, the more shapes and sounds it takes as in the philosophy of Judaism where G-d has several names, namely the name of fear, of wisdom, of intelligence and many others. Also, He has a name which evokes respect to such an extent that must not pronounce it, but must come to the point of thinking how it is mispronounced and thereby reaching beyond him.

The fact of the matter is that there exist two registers of languages: one in which we pronounce and produce sound, and the other: body language, the movements of which cannot deceive or lie. One of the most important usages in which body language is expressed, whereby the use multiple possibilities including gestures to emphasize the spoken word, while the main physical implements that express in action, the thoughts in the mind such as writing, using tools for work etc.

Before going too deeply into the subject of body language, it is first necessary to explain the theory of shapes and in particular the triangle. Almost everything has an overall shape, which in its simplest form could be described as a square, an oblong, a circle or a triangle.

In the human being the inner structure of the body appears to bear the triangular shape. The hands and feet are the ultimate tools of the human body, but on the surface they do not appear to be associated with any triangular shape. Let's obtain a deeper understanding of where the physical source that causes movement to these vital organs exists. We know of course that it is the brain that sends a signal and thereby causes the organs to respond, but there is a third element, which actually motivates movement in the hands and feet. The key that unlocks this mystery is to be found in the overall shape of the butterfly. The two top wings and the two lower wings are associated with our two shoulder blades and hip bones. The butterfly's body to which the wings are hinged can be related to our backbone. Our two shoulder blades direct movement to our arms and hands and our two hip bones direct movement to our legs and feet. Both are of triangular shape and are inverted with the angular sharp end, pointing downwards. A triangle which points downwards is substructure is opposed to the law of gravity and, therefore, enables us to be extremely mobile like a butterfly able to move from one flower to another; the human being can walk, run, jump, swim and perform amazing actions of mobility. At the same time a Yogi stands on his head which is similar to the inverted point of the triangle, thus reversing the action of gravity in order to concentrate and meditation spiritual thought as opposed to physical thought.

It would seem that in our everyday life, through our very gestures, we are unconsciously either attracting or rejecting gravity. When we think for instance, our hands often go to our heads as if to lighten the burden of gravity bearing us down on that encases our brain. Another common gesture is when we want to rid ourselves of something we dislike. We tend to carry out a brushing away action with the topside of the hand. This action is always downwards. In other words, we are throwing it back to gravity. Even in the relationship between human beings, such as shaking hands or kissing we use the upper part of the body and in this way, we signify that we want to unite our spiritual beings.

An important aspect of body language embodied in both gesture and touch, it is interesting to note, that if touching involves an upward movement it tries to be more connected to the spiritual plane. Yet, if the movement is downwards it is invariably physical and we are attempting to return to the Earth. To understand these gestures, it is necessary to analyze the ritual movements of various religions. One most interesting is the sign made by Roman Catholics and Greek Orthodox by hand movements signifying an overall shape of a triangle as the triangle is resting on its base. This is generally done at climactic moments when they are somehow involved or moved by spiritual thought. In the Jewish tradition, the fingers touching the two eyes by forefinger and thumb, and then moving downwards until the finger and thumb meet at the mouth produces the triangular movement. It would seem that if the gesture made signifies that the base of the triangle is upwards, there is a desire to obtain increased spiritual enlightenment, but on the other hand, if the base is downwards, the desire may be a search for something more physical. However, the gestures are eternally geared to either ascending or descending and cannot be separated, but are complementary. It would appear that in a human being, there is the unique desire to maintain a balance between the spiritual and physical plane and this is particularly focused in religious gestures.

The Chinese have crystallized this eternal aspiration of man to healing and acupuncture. This healing symbol which incorporates two enlarged "yods" that are interlinked. One named "YIN", the other "YANG". Both contain a small circle. The "INN" represents spiritual life and the "YANG" represents physical life. Therein always part of "INN" in "YANG" and "YANG" in "INN". This is conveyed both by the overall interconnection of the cods and by the two smaller circles that bring a part of "INN" in "YANG" and a part of "YANG" in "INN". This shows that the spiritual is interlinked to the physical and cannot be separated. One is as vital to man as the other and yet most religions are concentrated on one aspect of life and reject the other aspect, thereby denying the relationship without which the overall human structure could not coherently exist.

A further example of body language is clearly represented by a baby who is tired and with clenched hands makes an inward, circular movement towards its eyes, whereas an adult tends to make an outward movement with their hands away from the eyes. This means that the baby is trying to get all the elements of his structure into himself, whereas the adult is endeavors to do just the opposite. So, we must try to observe our actions in order to understand, not only the reason for particular gestures, but whether it is really what we are searching for. The fact of the matter is, we tend to concentrate all our attention on what we observe outside ourselves, rather than trying to understand ourselves through our instinctive modes of expression.

For instance, do we ever bother to study the overall shape of the palm of our hands or are we so involved in trying to discover our future from the lines therein, that we miss the most vital factor? This is the triangle, which is formed when both palms are placed together. This triangle points towards us and is like an open-ended arrow-head. It appears to be a sign directing us to seek the wisdom and enlightenment that lies within every one of us, but for some unknown reason some people place their palms together and cover up the triangle when praying. Also is it not a fact that if we showed our two linked palms to others, they would not be interested because the arrow points towards us and not them? Yet we shake hands in an attempt to communicate when we do not properly understand ourselves and, therefore, are hardly likely to understand the person to whom we are linking our hands. Instead, we communicate mainly in ignorance and often fill up a void with meaningless words. The truth being, we talk, talk, talk, without actually knowing the true meaning of what we are saying.

This brings us to another aspect of body language that refers to the mouth as a linguistic instrument. Most linguists concentrate solely on the structure and historical basis of a language, without any awareness of its movement and the overall shape of the instrument that allows the language to be spoken in the first place. Linguists often ignore of the very instrument that he works with. This instrument is designed out of a whole series of triangles, both in the tissue and bone structure and they are all positioned in a well thought out order, so that a whole range of sounds can be articulated. Shapes lead to movement and there is no other part of the human body that has such a cluster of triangles in such a small area as the human face. The top and bottom maxilla in which are rooted teeth, have a downward and upward movement which connects these two triangular shapes. The root of the tooth is a triangle, the tongue being the hinge that links up the upper palate to the lower palate and touches all the teeth. In order to talk we need to breathe and is it by chance that the nose is of triangular shape? The nose seems to be formed by facets of triangles linked to a triangle which rises from the two extremities of the upper lips to the top of the nose, where the eyes are positioned. So that it would appear that this forms triangles with one overall triangle. The jawbone represents another triangle which is attached to the overall triangle of the mouth and nose. Then there is the triangle of the cheeks which some women tend to highlight when using make up. This appears to be a continuation of the practice of highlighting the triangle of linguistic articulation on the cheeks by ancient Egyptians and some Red Indian tribes.

Once the overall structure of the face is studied in this manner, it is clear that the whole face is represented by a series of triangles joined together. This can especially be focused when a person smiles and clearly displays the triangles in the cheeks, mouth, nose and chin. Even the eyes, which appear to be circular are set in square orbits and their tear ducts are of triangular shape, so that even when we cry or laugh emotion is expressed from a triangle. The ear is shaped as a spiral and life comes from a spiral, the ultimate and overall shape of which is triangular. Also, at the base of the throat there is a triangle. It is interesting to observe that even when we deport ourselves, we form triangles in the movement of the forearm and biceps and when we walk a triangle is formed within each movement of our legs and thighs that opens and closes. This is also apparent when we nod our head, when we bend from the waist downwards and when we respond to music by tapping our feet. The triangle is also indicated when you spread your fingers.

A further fascinating indicator is found in the tongue. Have you ever opened your mouth and lifted up your tongue, turning it inwards? If you do, you will clearly see that as it folds there appears to your eyes two tissular triangles, hinged together. The one under the tongue pointing upwards, the other in your jaw pointing downwards.

The proof of the three-dimensional significance of the triangle unlocks itself step by step as we analysze this fascinating and unique seal, that our Creator has imprinted on to us. In this way we can seek knowledge as to our multi-dimensional self, which focuses towards unity of our three basic dimensions.

Chapter V
THE PROJECTION OF MAN

The question must be asked as to what extent is man different from the other living forms, which surround him? In the final analysis it seems that the only different dimension is in the tools and instruments that man has made and which serve him as a further extension of his hands. This extension appears in man's various activities in the context of work and leisure.

From a general point of view, in all man does he does not seem to have a basically different pattern from the various elements which constitute the world which surrounds him. The triangular seal is there, everywhere. Also, the "sign" of the animal world appears to be sealed by the triangular shape to various extents. A fly folds its legs, it has triangular shaped wings. The triangle is less apparent in the deportment of snakes, although they move by achieving different angles. The heads of certain types of dogs and other animals have a structure , which may equal man in the number of triangles they display. Their faces relate to the human face through a cluster of triangles.

As far as the vegetable world is concerned, the pattern of foliage appears in its unique design as a multiplication of segments branching off into different angles. In a way, the nerve pattern of leaves is similar to that of the nervous system of man. Even the tops of most leaves are pointed giving a general triangular shape. The same applies to the overall shape of most trees.

Two of the important differences that make man unique is first, man's fingers and, the opposite action of the thumb in relation to the fingers. The thumb seemingly activates the fingers and gives movement of the hand, balance and purpose. The fingers in conjunction with the thumb can make all kinds of shapes, from circles to other quadrilateral variations. Second, man seems to be able to produce a large range of sounds that are a synthesis of his experiences which will outlive him whereas although animals can record data and transform it into a personal performance, man can project further his novelties of ideas by more sophisticated associations using imagination and simulation.

Another aspect concerning the projection of man is his ability to use instruments that he has created in order to sharpen his various built-in articulation. The pen being the major instrument which sharpens up the triangle of thought giving it a finite outlook. When we use a pen we do not consciously consider the mechanics of its use. The whole philosophy of the writing movement is related to the way it fits into the hand. There is a close relationship between the output of thought and the by-product of the pen. It is interesting to note, that if you take an invisible line from the thought pattern in the head to the point of the pen, then the hand and arm which guides it, a triangle is formed with the base facing outwards, which gives the impression of a wide range of directions towards the forming of one's "wing".

The pen also requires two further resources before it activating ink and paper. There is a contrast between the color of the ink and that of the paper. (The inflexible shape of the pen and the mobility of the five fingers of the hand, arm and biceps follows the pattern of our thoughts either flexible or inflexible. At the same time, there is unity of action between the ink of the pen which empties itself onto the paper and the thoughts which take form and shape through the character of the letters formed). There are opposite forces used to hold the pen, the thumb being in contradiction to the fingers, although the compelling force moves the thumb towards the fingers. The pen coming from the base of a triangle formed between the base of thumb and forefinger goes through the point of the triangle and hence to the paper. This complex action is overlooked. Only the fact that we hold the pen seems to matter and we even forget we require an environment in which to write, a table, chair or a comfortable position. We do not stop to consider that there is a whole philosophy in the interaction of the movement. And yet, the pen has been the object, which has allowed man to project his ideas to think and communicate beyond his present environment and time. It is another "finger" to the hand and adds another dimension to our being.

When used for work it has allowed man to design and create other instruments and tools from the most "simple" hammer to "highly sophisticated" technology and this has allowed him to advance to an eternal cycle of life above and beyond any other known living form.

We are so engrossed in daily usage of various implements and consumption of various foods, either spiritual or material of different origins, that we don't even stop to consider that we, ourselves, are the main instrument that everything else revolves around. Perhaps because of this unawareness, we no longer really appreciate the results of our own efforts, the environment that surrounds us or even ourselves. We have even forgotten the meaning of colors and purpose of communication. Yet we long to create more and more tools and instruments, but the question is, why and for what purpose?

In order to answer this question, we should return to a further understanding of body language, particularly in the way we seek comfortable positions. One of the most common positions is when lying down we tend to place our hands behind our head with elbows extended, giving the impression that we wish to join our shoulder blades together and form one "wing type structure". The same applies to the thighs when squatting down cross legged. Both positions restrict body mobility, but increase comfort. The same applies when sleeping on our side. This has the effect of forming two "wings". One formed by our torso and the other by the thighs and legs.

In a human being there appears to be a conflict, in that we seem, in moments of sleep and relaxation, to want to transform ourselves into a one or two winged shaped entity, but at the same time and during those periods of work and activity, we seem to long to unclip those "wings" and go on producing, designing and creating more and more instruments and tools which will give us more and more "wings" that we can unclip at will.

In this respect, attention must be drawn to the fact that in ancient mythology it is not unusual to find that many of the mythical figures are portrayed as having wings. Angels in religion are also often portrayed with wings. It would appear that the human being in his or her unconscious state sees this as man in his most sublime and perfect state. Yet, because he seems to be driven to creating more and more implements including religious idols or rituals (other wings) there is the danger that his whole structure will become overloaded and that he will then deny his very existence and purpose. Instead of progressing towards a perfect and spiritual flight, he will ultimately regress into an animal status by losing his true identity.

Chapter VI
THE SEARCH FOR THE WING

The Wing or Wings represent the inner man, they are symbolic of house projects himself and form an integral part, not only of his physical structure, but of his philosophical and psychological attitude towards all that encompasses his life, both in his relationships with others, his work and his leisure and regulates his position in the cosmos.

As man has wings and antennae. So have nations, and the performance of these wings and antennae direct the position or structure of the man or nation in the overall scheme of things.

The Wing is that invisible dimension to the naked eye. It is nevertheless present by our daily actions, which prove that our wings not only exist in our subconscious mind, but are constantly used by us in body language. For instance, when we are scared of being hit, we raise our arm which is bent with elbow pointing upwards and even extend that shield by turning the thigh and knee inwards and raising one foot while remaining in a still position. The wing seems to have been transformed into a shield protecting us from harm.

Another example is when a mother is calling her children who are some distance from her. She gives a repetitive sign by folding her hand inwards as though she is pulling the children beneath her wing. Also the significance of the wing is seen when a mother or father places his or her arm around a child giving the impression of wrapping the wing around the child in love and protection. Children also tend to seek themselves to be enfolded in the Wing.

In religious blessing ceremonies with the placing of the hands by a minister on individual members of the congregation's heads give the same impression of the invisible wings enfolding and granting of benediction to the recipient. The movement applies also in faith healing.

It is interesting to note that when a king is crowned the Wings are much in evidence with the crown ascending and then descending towards the head of the monarch who all the time is protected by the Wings of the person who crowns him. To begin to analyse what the real significance of the Wing is, it is my intention to start at the point of searching for our own Wing. In this way the reader will be able to understand the full significance of the wing in relation to himself.

Wings can be defined as having six basic dimensions and cover every aspect of life. The first dimension involves a part of the body that, in conjunction with the tool or instrument, creates movement. The more sophisticated the implement, the fewer parts of the body it will involve. Also its shape and sophistication composing its mechanism will reflect its working capacity to produce more and more wings or objects. The fact is that sophistication has the effect of retracting the wings due to its almost automatic process denying man's natural skill and imaginations. It further has an almost soul-destroying process that relegates man to an automaton. These sophisticated machines invariably deny the triangular purpose of work and, therefore, deny man of his very purpose and being. He sees multitudes of objects (wings) being produced, but his reaction is to close his wings and therefore, he does not want to be fruitful and multiply.

Without body language, which incorporates the constant movement of our Wings, we stagnate and come under the law of inertia. The importance of movement cannot be stressed sufficiently as our whole life is ruled by moving from one cycle to another. There is the cycle of babyhood, that of infancy, that of childhood, adolescence (stressed by periods in women which work in cycles) manhood, old age etc. Also important are the clothes we wear, they follow the shape of our body, allowing for movement and action and are also an extension of our personality and character in that, as we evolve we change the design and fabric of our clothes, thus transforming the spectrum of our Wings.

The second dimension or Wing is to enable us to fly better and to become lighter. This means that we are able to communicate effectively and have a fuller understanding of the unified linguistic and body language of life.

The third dimension or Wing is a search for physical and spiritual direction. This search is achieved by ritual movements, some of which have been mentioned previously, and by other religious aids such as the symbols, saints and prophets, special buildings, clothes, incense, sounds and music. An example of body language in religion is seen at the Western Wall in Jerusalem. Worshippers bowing from the waist downwards like a bird pecking at food, which could be described as spiritual food with the worshipper, endeavouring to reach the antenna that would touch his wingspan to sharpen his ability to communicate.

Even people who are not religiously minded are bound to have poles of attraction, some of which are those mentioned above. It can be the strains of a particular piece of music, the painting or sculpture or an artist root message of a poet or writer. There is sufficient spiritual food for everyone to peck at. The search for the fourth wing is that of chance, beauty and poetry which leaves room for freedom of thought and taste although it seems from what we have studied so far that there appears to be little room for chance. There is a theory that there exists a tissular memory as well as a mental memory and during all our life we experience various shocks, which are imprinted on our inner memory. When we receive a physical blow from another person, the natural instinct is to retaliate, but when we hurt ourselves we just passively receive the effects of the injury and do not think to retaliate. In effect the shocks to our tissue accumulate and are stored in the tissular memory. This is because when we hurt ourselves by, say, bumping our leg against a chair, we do nothing in the way of expressing body language, whereas we should counteract the action by making an opposing movement with our other leg. In some ways our body language is instinctive, but in other ways it has to be consciously employed. However, if we consciously react against daily physical shocks, it would assist the tissular memory, but it would remove some of the mystery of our entity. Yet, even if we do not carry out the opposing movement, but think of it, it would sharpen the fourth wing without removing the poetry of man.

Beauty is dependent on our tissular memory and directs what we see as beautiful or ugly due to some shock or effect that has in the past imprinted itself in the memory. Nothing is by chance, all has a reason even though it is obscured from our consciousness. This is because our mental conscious memory bears no relation to our tissular memory which tends to supersede conscious thought, so that we either seem to instinctively appreciate beauty in a particular action or object or see it as ugly. It is the tissular memory which governs our reaction based on the hurts and shocks received in the past and accumulated in the memory and which directs our choice of beauty of poetry, music, painting, taste, etc.

In our search for the first antenna which concerns stimulation and drive we have to ask the question as to why we need to be so stimulated. Is it because of our lack of knowledge of the three-dimensional structure which necessitates a need to be impregnated with all kinds of different physical and spiritual stimuli? Or is it because we don't understand our resources, which already exist within us? All our artificial impregnations of drugs, alcohol, medicines etc. are only there to encourage the lie and create a feeling of well-being that does not exist deep within us, but simply lives on the surface and denies the wing of our essence and origin.

As to our search for the second antenna which concerns communication with G-d, it is first necessary to emphasize how difficult this is, because of the different religions and sects that have all become fragmented due to the breaking up of the triangle which was and still is basically within us. This has occurred due to daily consumption of adverse publicity not directed at unity, but towards fragmentation, which has inevitably hindered our direct communication with our Maker and taken away our original endowments such as telepathy, mind reading and the feeling of being part of the cosmos. And, has affected our vision of G-d as a concept which cannot be reduced down to a finite shape. Yet, this communication is within reach but because it is so beautifully simple and accessible, it is beyond our imagination. Everything is possible, everything is permitted, provided it complies with the Laws of Nature.

Chapter VII
SOME BASIC INSTRUMENTS OF THE WINGS

One of the most important basic instruments which is related to our first Wing concerns movement. Everything can be summed up or compared to the up and down movement of our jaws. In the same manner as we eat, consume, we stretch and move our Wings up and down thus consuming more and more of our environment, both moral, physical consumption and movement according to the complexity we reach. For example, let us consider the bicycle, which was created from the invention of the wheel. It involves circles: the two wheels, triangles: our two arms resting on the guiding bar and directing the instrument, our two legs and thighs pedaling, the overall mass of our muscles each of them being tied up and interlinked with an overall triangular shape. The brain is also involved both for balance, direction and giving signals to our limbs. Its shape is an overall circular shape. In nature the object which resembles it is the walnut. The skull itself is in perpetual movement. It is impossible to imagine the skull as being an immobile entity.

The mixture of triangular and circular shapes, which are involved in the means of transportation underlines mixed associations and purposes. The one difference which must be underlined is when the sources of energies other than man's mass of muscles are needed as the main source of energy. Planes, cars, boats, usually need fuel, thus reducing the triangular shape which involved man, but at the same time extending housing by extending the distance that can be covered. Again, a whole philosophy and outlook of these instruments of transport can be discovered by reducing them down to geometrical shapes.

The basic instruments of the Wing are those that help towards the flight once the four Wings and the antenna have been coordinated by each basic instrument which relates to one particular area within the butterfly outline.

When using these instruments, we can be on our own yet moving. Traveling in a car particularly allows this, we can be left with our thoughts while in movement. Thought can be a triangle in its own right and movement compared to a wheel rolling on. Other instruments not only involve movement, but also involve thought and skill, this applies both in work and leisure. A good example of movement in our leisure activity is dancing. A couple dancing and twirling towards a center pivot moves into a oneness. At first there appears a conflict between the spiritual and physical and this reflection in movement continues until unity responding to the music involved is reached. The dance is body language and communication unified as one, as unique mode of expression. Primitive dance used to be performed on one's own without a partner before it was transformed into a social occasion generally involving two people. In most discos, dances are now performed without a partner being required, which underlines a return to the origins of dance. However, the most intriguing recent event in modern dancing is the break dance, in which the dancer does not use his feet and legs, but his brain and skull as his base. He twists and rolls on the head, using the spine to bring in the movement. At the same time, the axis has not changed. The difference is that the head has become a physical rather than a spiritual pole of man.

Another example is that of wind surfing. This sport stresses individuality and involves many elements such as standing on the board, controlling the triangular sail,

Some Basic Instruments of the Wings

consciously searching for the wind, sailing on the water and the movement of the body which controls the entire instrument. In wind surfing you can see clearly how the triangular shape of the Wing (instrument) is involved in all its aspects including the elements of air and water, conveying three-dimensional movement. Also, how man by his thought pattern controls the Wing until he becomes part and texture of it. Yet the balance is very brittle, because without skill, feeling and understanding of the elements the sail loses its structural balance and man is thrown into the water. The instrument and man are then parted. But man has two Wings (arms) which he uses in the water, so although he has lost one structure, he is able to use another.

In wind surfing it is possible to see the beauty and poetry of man within his Wings which enable him, regardless of his activity, to change his structure to the Wing most suitable to his needs of movement and thought. This is the same with all the instruments he uses whether it be a hammer or a computer. If all the elements are not interconnected and one of the elements fail to conform to the general movement, then the structure breaks down and man becomes disorientated and heads for disaster until he, through suffering, relearning and experience, regains conscious equilibrium again.

Another basic instrument concerns communication. The telephone is a good example of this being a two-way communication system input and output and permits man to communicate over long distances and extend his linguistic Wing. Yet the telephone does not permit visual contact and because of this, it is not possible to obtain visual reaction to the spoken word. On the other hand, the telex only transports the written word and is even more impersonal. Radio is similar to the telephone, it projects the spoken word, but without visual contact cannot be completely personal. Television that incorporates visual and the spoken word tends to deceive and is in the main artificial and projects its own deceptive thoughts, which are impersonal and take away imagination and concentration. It would appear then that the telephone, radio and television to a lesser or greater extent make the input and output factor of communication more difficult. Only by person-to-person confrontation can true communication between human beings be properly established. This is because the senses of perception, feeling instinct and body language cannot be passed on by a machine. In this regard we seem to be so reliant on the machines of communication, that we overlook the possibility that there exists a far more perfect system, whereby all forms of communication both input and output between human beings is recorded. This system is established by our Creator since the beginning.

Our daily life on Earth is regulated by statistics, forms, letters and other records, such as birth, marriage and death. Even when we visit an auditor a record is kept of the prescription given. The telex is a ghost line of the telephone, so is it not possible that there exists a ghost line to the spoken and written word? This imprint could well be recorded along lines which we are not aware of, but which records not only our spoken words, but even our deepest thoughts thereby providing a much more potent and effective record of our experiences and activity on Earth than a man-made record. In this way there would be no void in accordance with the natural scheme of things.

Another important instrument of the Wing is the search for physical and spiritual direction, which will give balance, so that he can use the basic instruments at his command and, by flapping his Wings, attempt to attract one particular aspect of life which appeals to him. The aids he uses to obtain spiritual consciousness are the dimensions of symbols, sounds and music, but this is also so of the physical where each one of the dimensions can represent movement in one form or another.

As with ritual movements in various religions, the reason for which we do not understand, so it is with physical movements linked or not linked with instruments. We do these movements automatically and because they are instinctive and not prescribed, we do not think that perhaps one day this form of gesture which we do to form a cobweb, will slowly become more and more defined and will then be part of the essential structure of human understanding.

The spider is programmed to construct a perfectly formed cobweb, but if the process is interrupted, the spider is unable to continue and has to commence again from the beginning. At the present moment, in the constructing of our own cobwebs we seem to be like the spider, in that we do not understand the meaning of our activity. Yet we feel superior to the spider, because we consider that we can complete most of our unfinished activities. But with enlightenment, will we want to carry on that which was done in comparative ignorance or will we, with this new knowledge, desire to begin at the beginning?

For example, a singer conveys a message through melodious sound, yet may not be fully aware of how far the vibration is going to impress an individual, bringing him a new knowledge which could be overpowering for that individual who is not ready to receive it at his stage of evolution. For instance, it could be that John Lennon's assassination was due to an over-reaction to the pulsation and message conveyed in his music. The same might have applied to Kennedy's death and even to that of Jesus, in that the vibration contained in the message was too strong for some people's ability to handle it.

In most religious rituals, the triangular shape of the Wing has been clearly outlined and it is of no importance whether the triangle is pointing downwards or upwards, providing the triangles link so that oneness is reached, thereby avoiding the necessity to kill in order to avoid uncontrollable vibrations and disharmony.

Chapter VIII
Double Standards

Man in his praise of G-d consciously or unconsciously is thanking the Creator for taking him out of the void and giving him life. By putting melodic sound in our prayers when praising G-d, man is giving more shape and filling more of the void by his own spiritual consciousness. This is due to the sound coming from his inner self being expressed outwardly from that which lies deep within his soul, this being the very fire, water and air of himself which is the three-dimensional image in the three-dimensional elements surrounding him.

When G-d breathed life into us in order to bestow upon us a living soul, we understood the full meaning and purpose of ourselves through our direct communication with G-d.

It seems that we have, through our obsession with the material and physical elements of our structure, dimmed this link with G-d. This can only be revived by reaching human emancipation and the first step towards this is by the true understanding and full meaning of the sounds we utter, together with our knowledge of the unified theory of the triangle, leading to the enlightenment of the ritual and body language gestures performed bus.

Although language is basically like any other instrument, man did not totally create it himself and is still unable to fully comprehend its complexities. Therefore, the linguistic instrument resembles an open-ended triangle of immense depth shrouded in mystery. Human emancipation cannot come from the creation of more and more instruments of communication, but from within man's own potential and his understanding of his double standards within his inner structure. The difference between the physical and the moral appears as a double standard which needs no explanation. But on the other hand, have we ever thought that there could be a double standard both within the physical and spiritual side of man, one being with reasoning and the other not involved with reasoning, yet both are within the physical and moral structure. As an example, a mother feeds her baby without reasoning as this is an integral part of the moral and physical aspect of nature, but when the baby grows into a child and needs to be guided, then the mother uses her power of reasoning in a moral context.

Also, when Peter Pythagoras drew up a triangle in order to put forward his theory, he used reasoning, but when he could not think of any ideas to put forward and was still holding a pen above a piece of paper, he might have done some doodles as if to compensate for the void in his mind. This latter action was not reasoning. Both actions produced a drawing, one was a superficial object, the other a natural object. Only a man could see the difference of the source of energy used to undertake the drawings. However, the doodles were finally part of the whole process which led to the finalizing of his theory. The natural sources are an integral part of the superficial one.

So far, man has concentrated on understanding the final product obtained by reason and ignored the other facets involved. When we decide to stop and analyse the unthinkable facet of man (doodles for instance) we shall reach a much higher level of understanding not only of ourselves and of body language but also of the spoken word.

At the present moment we consider that there is a difference between a beehive, which is a natural object, and a computer, which we consider an artefact. But have we considered that when making a computer we go through a lot of unreasoned actions such as smoking cigarettes, drinking coffee, gossiping, etc. that, in fact, had nothing to do with the construction of the computer. Yet, the bees solely concentrate on their allotted task, so that in the last analysis, the computer appears to be more of unnatural object compared to a beehive, which does not appear as an artefact. It seems then, that we only accept the computer as a finished object and reject the other side of the coin of man which played an equal part in the elaboration of the final product. This is the part of our living soul which is totally ignored and to which we should try to focus more attention.

In order to grasp a little better this hidden side of man one must give more examples.

For instance, a woman has just visited a friend, they had a drink, a discussion, some food. When the visit is over, the person leaves the house, walks to the car. On the way there are some trees, some of its branches overhang the pavement. The woman might take no notice of the overhanging branches as she walks past, but she might take a leaf which she either keeps or crumbles in her fingers and throws it away. In both these cases, the tree was there as part of her tissular memory and the taking of a leaf by the woman is an action to be analysed. It can be summed up as filling a void just as the discussion with her friend filled up a similar void. Both are related to consumption. Many of our daily gestures relate to this type of action that guides our lives. For instance, why do we decide to wear a blue pair of trousers today or why do we prefer to consume an apple at night rather than in the morning when we may prefer to drink orange juice? Is it through mimesis or is it uncontrolled action?

We often think that flowers have a language of their own, but we do not try to read our own language nor the language of fruits, we simply leave our unrelated gestures and shapes to chance. And, at the same time, although we try to give a meaning to flowers, we stop short of giving meaning to ourselves. This tends to give the impression that we consider ourselves as being of a lesser entity than some of the vegetable world.

There are two possibilities, either our "unrelated" actions are guided by another power outside ourselves or the "unrelated" actions are fully controlled by ourselves. Do both possibilities have a purpose? All actions are supposed to be part of the essential project e.g., the survival of the species and these "unrelated" or illogical actions whether we accept it or not are part of that project. There is no void, everything is meaningful, even actions which seem to have no real purpose. Newton discovered his theory of the law of gravity by observing an apple, which fell in front of his eyes – by chance. This particular apple made history, not all apples will have the "chance" to fall in front of such a sharp eye. It would appear then that when something of this nature occurs, it is not totally by chance, but by design. Simple details are often the cause, which sparks off union between human beings from the friendship level to the marriage level. This also applies to employment and to many other leisure activities involving a number of people. An impulsive, affectionate act towards another person, such as the sending of flowers or of greeting cards gives pleasure both to the sender and the receiver. It crystallizes a spiritual bond. But even this simple act can have double standards, in that the motive may be completely self-motivated. Yet, the flower or gift in fact is no different in its shape than the beehive and the computer because everything is connected and basically stems from impulse. It is not only because of his theoretical and medical background that a psychiatrist discharges his patient from hospital after one or more consultations but because of a few little nothings. A simple gesture such as the crossing of a leg, a softer vibration in the voice, a smile which came at a crucial moment and a whole series of added up elements, which guide the doctor to decide that the patient is no more a patient, but a complete individual whose Wing has been repaired so that he can be freed from the confinement of the hospital and fly freely again, until other details will attract him to a different pole and again his Wing will not be impervious to the influences of other man-made structures which will cause further damage to his Wing.

Psychiatric hospitals are currently full of men and women who do not respond to any particular pole of attraction except that of their own. Their reactions do not appeal to those who are regulated by a pole because they are without inhibitions and, often act contrary to a socially accepted standard of normality. As an example, a woman who constantly changes her clothes during the day, is expressing the fact that she has not yet found her own pole which will suit her skin. Pills might temporarily change her direction, but in the final analysis they will only delay her "problem". Pills will lead her to immobility, which is just the opposite of the need expressed by her body. Only through movement will she find her own balance.

Most people in prisons are people on the move. They have moved in order to survive either by following a smile, glance or a packet of cigarettes, until the general movement did not appeal to the other movement of men, who again tried to force them to be immobile. The climactic, moment, which emphasizes this mobility by force rather than by pills, is when the future prisoner is being suddenly manacled. By this action his Wings are knotted together, so that he will be tied to a pole until he reaches the other pole, which regulates the movement of "normality". But has anyone seen a man being manacled? Has anyone looked into his eyes and seem how his soul flies away from restrictions of his corporal structure. Movements towards the right direction will never occur unless it is willingly accepted with one's heart and soul.

Man can never be made immobile no matter what the circumstances. He must move eternally so that complete stillness, even after death, is not conceivable in the general structure of nature. Yet many men try to restrict movement and even force restraint through various means such as man-made laws, medication and excessive commercialism. When one way communication does not go far enough to destroy and annihilate the movement of the mind, because the body still moves instinctively following its natural pole, then destructive weapons of all descriptions are used as a last resort to further and put a final stop to free movement unaccepted by one side of the coin of the human race.

Double standards are the stimuli which lead a man to follow one direction and yet look at the opposite direction and will perhaps finally prevent him from following his nose so that he achieves the opposite to what he had contemplated to do in the first place. Double standards are the ultimate free choice that, through a process of direction, can branch off towards the reverse side. The final answer not being programmed by any source of influence, except the one that leads the butterfly shape we resemble, to bounce from one flower to another or from one pole to another.

The ultimate freedom being so unfettered that it longs to be restrained by some kind of overwhelming force and at the same time longs to be released from any such force whether it is hate, love, indifference or sympathy. In fact, in this double-bladed search, freedom longs for unity and communication at all levels, particularly in communication with our ultimate Maker who gave us countless other inner resources for our use. Such communication is not hard to achieve, in that it is not theoretical. It can be obtained by any man who has been able to link knowledge and instinct through his daily actions.

Some people will never be able to find their own pattern of daily life. Hence they will follow the pattern of someone who seems to have achieved it. He might be named Buddha, Karl Marx or Mohammed, but in the final analysis, man will be given many other opportunities until he finds his own pattern or until his pattern follows the intelligent pattern of the universe.

It is written in the palm of our hands, in the shape of the bones, which govern our movements, in the design and colour of an apple, orange, a carrot, or a banana. Other mirrors reflect the same triangular message and can readily be deciphered if one takes the time to stop and decipher it. It is all part of the universal language, which is so much in front of our eyes that we, because of its closeness, are blind to its reality. Perhaps if it had been given in a more mysterious style, it could have been the centre of our focus and we would have diligently sought out the simple message it contained and so reached emancipation instead of creating complex and complicated philosophies that still evade the truth. Until then humanity will still be crying out for external solutions and smother the inborn search.

Chapter IX
Removing the Outer Shell of Man

Man, although he is unaware of his own actions, has erected around himself a shell and in doing so, denies his very existence as an entity within the cosmos. He only sees what he wants to see and restricts himself to a single dimension. His reason for doing so can be twofold, in that he either considers himself superior to the cosmos or he is afraid to recognize his true self, because it is unknown to him and he is reluctant to break out of the shell that encompasses him. So let us make an attempt to break into the shell and understand what exists at the core. For this purpose, it is intended to concentrate on the visual aspect and in this way, it will be possible to gain a glimpse of that which exists behind the shell. So let us focus our attention on three main aspects of graffiti.

The first being, when a man or woman is concentrating on a particular subject or conversation they doodle unconsciously on a piece of paper. Usually, they nearly always perform the same doodle over and over again, as if they are programmed to sketch that particular doodle and no other. All people do it regardless of their profession, trade or station in life and to focus on that aspect is to focus on an essential facet of human life.

Usually there is a movement conveyed by the doodle, which

is, in fact, as mobile as life itself. This is the first element. The second element is the opposition of movement and this is immobility and life revolving around stillness. Sometimes there is a third element, which can be analysed in a different way depending on the doodle. Generally, doodles are made of geometrical shapes, but there are no general patterns in the human soul, so that some people do not solely draw circles, ovals, squares and oblongs, but may draw animals, faces etc., which are basically made out of geometrical shapes.

Since one cannot analyse particular doodles case by case, individual by individual, we shall now concentrate on the second category of doodle which have become so popular that they are known worldwide as symbols. The first example is the symbol of the Olympic Games. It is made up of five circles interlinked with each other. Three being above and two being below. Some people are aware that they represent five continents, others see an idea of a linkage, but few are those who want to analyse further. Let us try to understand how this symbol came to be designed. Usually, every small firm has a small insignia which tries to convey the message of the purpose of the business, so when the Olympic symbol was designed, it was perhaps created for a similar kind of purpose. Another possibility is that it was only the doodle or graffiti of one individual, which caught on and reached universal popularity.

There are five rings, five fingers in a hand and five continents. Our life seems to work through the cycle of the figure five and to reach its utmost efficiency when the five elements are interlinked, so that they can all work towards the same movement. Why have circles been selected rather than other shapes? A ring fits over a finger, meridians fit on to continents and around the globe; the circle is also the primitive shape of the cell, the shape, which cannot lie.

Although the Olympic Games focus on physical life, the spiritual aspect is not rejected as shown by the three circles above which might represent it, as opposed to the two circles below which might represent physical life. Whatever it is, the main point, is that both are linked one to the other. Further, the circles each represent a basic colour and if mixed represent all the colours of the national flags in the world. So there exists three dimensions, shape (circles), colours and movement through linkage.

Another graffiti which has a profound effect on man and which goes back to antiquity, yet covers all aspects of life e.g., power, peace, health politics and commerce, is the caduceus: the wand carried by ancient Greeks or a Roman Herald, also the wand of Hermes the Winged G-d.

According to legend the wand of Hermes became a symbol of peace and concord. And since Hermes was also the G-d of commercial transactions, the caduceus became the insignia of commerce. It was also attributed to other gods such as Bacchus who had made peace between various other gods. In all these cases it became a symbol of peace and, as a consequence, the Greeks gave this emblem to ambassadors and all those charged with peace missions.

This emblem has become the official insignia of the medical profession. The emblem is shown as a wand surrounded by one or two serpents and at each end of the wand there are Wings, which have nowadays been stylised as triangles. There are many possible interpretations. The wand can be our spinal column, our hinge or axis, to which are fitted our two Wings, e.g., legs and arms. The serpents could be associated with our antennae which bring life and stimulation. Another interpretation focuses on the fact that the top triangle has a larger area than the lower triangle. The larger triangle points downwards and might be that of spirituality similar to the shoulder blade, which directs our hand. The small triangle rests on one of its bases and the whole weight of gravity coming from above seems to crash through the wand or vertebral column into the small triangle. The whole weight of the body is held on the structure that rests on the iliac, i.e., the upper part of the hip bone.

Another interpretation is that the large triangle downwards represents all the illnesses while the small triangle pointing upwards is the progress achieved by medicine and sciences from the illnesses coming from above that were some of the reject products that followed creation.

The third element, serpent or serpents entwining the wand from top to bottom beyond the top triangle, demonstrates that the law of gravity can be overridden. The serpent may be the hand of man represented either by the doctor or by the patient himself if he is able to take charge of himself. Also, the serpent can represent the different aspects of the medical science. It also appears from this movement that man, with his hand, by wanting to override gravity, adds extra gravity. The essential ascending movement goes so far that it falls down onto itself. From this, it seems that, in the final analysis, medicine can add to medical problems. This is displayed from the final movement downwards as opposed to the initial movement upwards.

Sometimes, the caduceus insignia is more stylised. It represents one snake entwining one single triangle but the final message conveyed remains basically identical.

Apart from the caduceus symbol, many others contain a message akin to a sigh, a breath of air releasing the overflow of energy, which needs to find an outlet. One of them is the five-pointed star used for instance in the American flag. In this particular case where each single star represents one state, we have an accumulation of various hands all tied together towards the building of a nation.

Religious symbols have been selected out of thousands in order to convey a concept capable of entering the inner reaches of man and create a safety valve balancing the overflow of energy between the spiritual and physical dimensions. Basically, all the symbols emerge from the circle, which responds to primitive sources and impulses and with time the circle becomes sharper and more defined until it is transformed into another shape.

Let us consider the Christian cross, which is made out of two wands one vertical with the other crossing it horizontally in an unequal distance from the top of the upright wand to the bottom. The two wands connect, which is the original core of the original circle (cell). Later this produced the physical and spiritual life, which were a larger part of the same entity, but had become separated. However, the link remained at the point of connection where the upright wand was crossed by the horizontal wand. So, in the beginning there was a concentration of energies which became expanded, so there is in the cross a movement of contraction and a movement of expansion. Should imaginary lines be drawn from point to point on the cross it produces four triangles. These triangles still represent the search for increased communication through enlightenment. They are also the four Wings of the butterfly, with the upright wand being the hinge or body of the butterfly. However, one notices that on first sight the antennae is missing, but if the imaginary line is continued upwards it not only produces the antennae by an open-ended triangle, but this is applicable to both ends. The number of Wings (instruments for knowledge and communication) can always be extended.

The next symbol is that of the Muslim faith, which is the crescent of the moon. Again, it is derived from the circle (full moon). There also exist two triangles of imaginary lines, which are drawn close to the two points of the crescent. It is also like a little embryo, which is contracted and able to expand. An embryo includes everything within it, so that it contains all the elements of the butterfly shape.

In Buddhism the symbol is represented by a flower which Buddha himself favoured personally. This flower contains a heart (cell) surrounded by petals and leaves – expansion of the concentrated embryo again through the triangle shape (Wings).

In Judaism the most ancient religious symbol is a candelabra with seven candle-holders, but in the eighteenth century there appeared the Star of David made out of two triangles linked to each other, one pointing downwards and the other pointing upwards. It could be that the triangle pointing downwards represented oriental philosophy and the one pointing upwards occidental philosophy. As both triangles are linked together, it is like returning to the circle by using the two triangles. So, in analysis we have the concentration – circle, expansion – two triangles searching for concentration. Within the Star of David there are six triangles and the heart, so there is a connection between the Star of David and the candelabra. To me, the connection is twofold: first of all, the multiplicity which is part of the Law of Nature being the central point of nature and second, the link between all the philosophies. In the Star of David, the only two philosophies are depicted. These fragment into other philosophies once they are linked with its seven branches. There are also seven built-in philosophies without transformation, all capable of being lit up, thence from this unique and philosophical base they unite into one light. The figure seven is a symbol, which is associated with repetition, e.g., seven days etc.

Similar to all the other symbols, the candelabrum of Judaism has the butterfly shape in that the four lower branches represent the four Wings, the two upper branches the antennae and the centre upright to which the branches are attached being the hinge of body of the butterfly. This symbol has another dimension in that it originates from a base of a root giving fertility to the branches and energy to the lights at the tip of the branches; all stem from the root and branch outwards into a multiplicity of philosophies enlightening communication and knowledge.

Another interesting factor about the ancient candelabrum symbol of Judaism, is that it also represents air, water and fire; the branches reaching upwards into the air, the watering of the branches so that they can grow, with the water descending to the base to create fire. These three elements represent the light by the air, the water being fertility and the fire, which can only exist in the air. The soul being the fire of the spirit.

In the other symbols, it is assumed that the above exists in the embryo, but in the ancient symbol of Judaism this is clearly depicted.

Having analysed some of the religious symbols, which are similar to a sign language which tries to give the essence of a philosophy, let us now concentrate on another form of sign language which may appear more down to earth but which in fact relates to the same overall pattern defining geometrical shapes, for instance, road signs. There are three main shapes on which the signs are depicted to draw attention to road users. The three shapes used are triangles, rectangles, squares and circles. All signs giving orders are circles with one exception, the "Yield sign. All warning signs are in triangles and all direction and information signs are within squares and rectangles. So here again the primitive cells just respond to orders and are shown by circles. The more elaborate triangular shape, which implies more articulation giving warning signs and the direction and information signs, which appeal to human choice and thought are shown by the square or rectangular shape. There is only one interesting exception which it is necessary to point out and that is, all the warning signs are triangles resting on a base pointing upwards with only two of them pointing downwards.

By this it will be seen that driving a car is very much related to gravity, therefore, all the signs except two are resting on a base, rather than resting on the point (head). The only signs resting on the head relate to a "Give Way" or a "Stop" sign.

The language of colour would appear to play a large part in projecting road signs. The red colour which is clearly associated with blood and therefore danger is connected with the important purpose of stopping or slowing down movement forward. On the other hand, the green and blue colours can be associated with water and sea. They lead to movement and are in most cases used with the arrow signs implying movement.

In spite of such a large diversity of shape and movement, the same theme occurs again and again, leading to unity through apparent fragmentation.

Chapter X
THE INNER SHELL OF MAN

Man has always expressed himself in shapes in that he is fascinated, distressed or frustrated by them. He admires and sees the beauty of some shapes and rejects others as being repulsive. His emotions are governed to a large extent by their visual representation, which he can fear and attempts to destroy. He also can express love, beauty and joy by images and shapes, which he continually sees around him, yet he is rarely fully conscious of their significance and impact.

For example, people cannot mourn someone unless they are able to represent the image of that person in their mind. If there is no image there exists a terrible void, which has to be filled in order to obtain balance. For instance, the Unknown Warrior symbolizes many deaths and casualties in war, which cannot be visualized as a whole. This represents something finite in people's minds and creates an image to fill what would otherwise be a void. This is also supported by a religious service paying homage to an unknown shape or image in order to give it more purpose and shape.

In the Roman Catholic Church there exists many images of the Virgin Mary and her son Jesus. These images are made as beautiful and artistically attractive as possible so that the adherents to Catholicism can express themselves through a material image that they can see, in order to fill a void that might otherwise exist. The interesting fact these displays in churches may help the Roman Catholic religion to appeal and therefore to retain large congregations. It would seem therefore that man needs images and shapes that he can see and understand in order to provoke an emotional response. It could be said that popes are also charismatic images who draw a large response from large crowds.

In the theory of osteopathy, it is known that usually the position of comfort goes towards the lesion. For instance, if somebody has pain in his back, his most comfortable position would be to lie on his back and place all his weight on it. The same would apply in order to explain the need for images of the Virgin Mary and the pope; as if the spiritual illness is because G-d appears without image. Therefore, it would seem that the creation of images is a sign of pain which has not yet been cured in many people, to such an extent that there are those who even deny the existence of G-d. Yet, there are around us an immense accumulation of signs and shapes that He has left behind Him without a patent, but most people are more concerned with what He has not left – a human image of himself.

The human race being what it is, with no one person agreeing or exactly seeing the same as another, it would appear that if G-d had left an image of himself, this could have meant joy to some, but antipathy to others. Therefore, He left a visionless concept where everyone can create within themselves the shape and image of how they see their Maker.

Judaism is not a religion of the image although it includes some symbols previously analysed. The symbol of the Star of David was, however, a sufficient image to spark off the violent hatred of some men. For instance, the hatred that Hitler displayed towards Judaism was crystallized in his own graffiti, which he drew as an antidote against what he called poison e.g., Jewish philosophy. The borrowed Nazi insignia clearly displays a self-contained clockwise movement, a cell revolving around itself without communication with another cell, therefore producing infertility and stagnation. The "light", which is focused by this graffiti focused his own lesion: the impossible dream of any cell consisting in becoming two cells. His inner self rejected the Star of David for all that it represented; communication with other cells. Because of this and his unsuccessful attempt to fill his own void, he devised death and destruction as the only means to heal his own structure, which, in the end, due to the misshapen shape and image He created, effectively produced His own demise.

The shape of survival can also be vitally important and in this respect, gestures which appear as trifles in normal existence take a climactical dimension when survival is at stake. Let us give the example of Samuel Pisar's mother who was in a concentration camp with her son following the temporary success of Hitler's creed. On one particular day, she had to decide whether she should dress her son with shorts or with trousers. She deduced through an instinct of survival that he should wear trousers, so that in a group of men he would appear as a man and thus be sent to work with the men rather than stay with the children who were considered to be parasites and therefore doomed to death. Because of her well thought out gesture, this man is still alive and became a very successful international lawyer.

To understand the inner shell of man, it is perhaps vital that we deal with one of the main aspects which involves him in daily life, that of consumption. In order to understand how we consume and what we consume and why it involves knowledge, it is necessary to start at the beginning with a baby in the womb of its mother. This is a simple two-way relationship with the movement of life passing between mother and baby. The quality of the food depending on the mother's consumption. The food enters the mother's mouth, is passed down to the stomach and, after chemical processes, nourishment is passes to the baby. Waste from mother and baby is passed through the intestines and out of the body. The movement of consumption and rejection can be depicted by two open sided triangles, which have the overall shape of a flash of lightning with two oblique lines joined up and separated by a smaller line which symbolically and philosophically depicts the force of life produced by the mother. At the same time, the mother creates a triangular movement while she consumes her food. But before consumption, has she given any thought as to the specific food she eats? Whether she has or not will make a considerable difference both at her level and within the human chain of life.

After the fetal stage, follows consumption through suckling. A baby who sucks his mother absorbs a part of the learning of life. The mother by giving a part of her substance also and by taking part of a substance external to herself, also absorbs some of this knowledge. She has a feeling both of well-being and pain. The well-being is by giving part of herself to her creation and the pain is the one that she feels, during the first phases of breast feeding, when the vagina retracts itself while the baby sucks from her. She feels a triangular pain, which originates from the lower part of her vagina and simultaneously goes up towards the right and left ovary ducts. Is it also due to chance, that there is a triangular movement in the pain itself which gives life at the particular organ that fertilizes life i.e., the ovaries?

After the suckling comes the weaning of the baby from the mother's breast. In primitive societies the mother would chew the food and introduce it directly from her mouth to the baby's mouth like birds that carry out the same movement from beak to beak. When a spoon is used instead of the mouth, mother sits baby on her lap in the crook of her arm and feeds the baby with her other arm. In both case it involves a triangular movement when the mother carries the food with her hand, whether it is towards her mouth or the baby's mouth, but the triangle is less sharp in the first case of mouth-to-mouth feeding. In both cases the baby would lie in the crook of her arm thus forming a circle so the circular and the triangular movements appear more complex as life develops and as another triangle appears with the father's presence.

Apart from material food there is also the emotive food in this three-way relationship, if the atmosphere is amicable, then the emotive shock is diluted. So when the baby is big enough, the chair or the floor might replace the lap; the mother or the father would provide another triangular movement when taking the food from the container. And, then another widening up triangular movement occurs in order to introduce the food. The circle of the arm holding the child has disappeared, there remains only repetitive triangular movements until the meal is finished. Therefore, the only circle that remains is that of the child closing up the family unit. Different movements translate different states of childhood. As we evolve into adulthood, triangular movements through consumption become more involved with the use of instruments, spoon, fork, knife etc. The triangular movements completed by our biceps and hands carry on all the way though, from the purchase of the food by looking for some cash in the purse or in the wallet to the extracting of food from the soil, bushes or trees, and this movement even applies to the slaughtering of animals for human consumption, up to the stage when food is served at the table.

In a modern society people are not so discerning in what they eat and are more engrossed in consuming so that they do not give any thought to the overall shape and structure of what they consume.

For example, has one ever considered an orange and fully observed its structure? It has a thick skin, flesh, juice and seed, and its colour is linked to that of the sunshine. It usually has ten slices and its flesh invigorates and is particularly revitalizing. An apple on the other hand has a thin skin, its flesh is not separated out by slices. An artichoke has a multiplicity of leaves and one heart, which can be eaten after removing all the leaves. Some parts are edible, some are not and the same applies to a banana. Yet, in the case of meat, most people consume it wholly without considering that it has a carcass, that some parts should be rejected and some other parts consumed. Other people think that some of the animals we consume have a soul linked to the Creator. Thus, when consuming meat we are in effect consuming a portion of that soul. Is it not essential then that we do not consume those parts of the animal's body that would influence our own soul and, therefore, reduce the flight of our own "Wings"? So, has anyone considered that the animal from which we get beef is formed with a top part and a lower part like a human being? The truth of the matter is that we simply consume without caring where or what and which design produced our food. This is especially so today with so much food being processed. We do not seem concerned as to the shape of the animal as for instance, whether it has a split hoof and yet the hoof is a clue as important as the hand of a human being, which provides the animal with locomotion and direction.

Whereas we make laws concerning almost everything, in so far as the animals we eat are concerned, there is a gap, which reflects on our knowledge or lack of knowledge relating to the philosophy of Nature. By doing so we do not divide our physical part of life or our moral aspect of life. We become uncoordinated instruments and fail to see the light, which shines through all the darkness that surrounds us. It is strange that we go on consuming without giving a thought as to what we eat, yet when we read a book we absorb its contents and generally are trained to make it our business to understand what we are reading. We select, we classify and we reason. So there appears to be a discrepancy and lack of linkage between our physical consumption and our spiritual consumption. Both have their effects on an individual, yet with the spiritual aspect we adopt one particular attitude, which might alter our direction, whereas with the physical aspect we fail to recognize that there could be an equally important influence on us.

As well as moving our jaws up, down and sideways to eat we also use our jaws and mouth to talk. For example, at a business dinner or at a luncheon or meeting of important members of a government around the meal table, not only do the participants eat, but they also talk and make important decisions. It follows that it is impossible to understand the core of man unless a complete understanding of consumption is obtained, because food enters the structure of man and is broken down to the very life force that motivates him, even to the way he thinks and acts. However, at political luncheons one-dimensional man leaves the processing of food down to the body and lets his mind focus on other issues that he considers as being of larger importance. Is our lack of discernment relating to physical consumption because the same instrument (mouth) is used for both purposes (eating and talking)?

Although most men and women do not realize that part of their inner core is expressed through consumption and rejection, some do admit that work reflects a part of their inner self. There are two possibilities. Either a person finds a work rewarding and considers the achievement obtained as a projection of himself or herself or only considers work as a means of subsistence. In this latter case, one might not even wonder whether one's work is or is not fulfilling. Whether a person works in an assembly line or is in the writing profession is irrelevant: the worker in an assembly line because of his mechanical gestures, the journalist because he has to cover a topic, which is of no genuine interest to him.

The projection of man appears to vary according to the working instrument. The more an instrument is sophisticated the least it will allow an individual to express himself and the more triangles he will spiritually give up. The more basic the instrument the more physical triangles he will need to produce from within himself and release at the same time some of his spiritual triangles through the physical channel. Whether physical movement can be linked with spirit is not always relevant. A gardener can think and work as opposed to a factory machinist. Yet, he may not be totally fulfilled because he has to do this work for mere survival rather than from choice. It appears that the drawing line is frail regardless the instruments concerned. The main aspect to be considered is whether a particular work fits the spiritual and physical movement of the core of a particular individual. In our modern society it appears that very little room is left for this kind of consideration so that when moving at work man gives up more and more of his physical entity and of his soul. This results in the danger of fragmenting a large part of his inner core, which is hidden by consumption and rejection. Any of these aspects can be fragmented or shrouded by another one or others that seem to fulfil him so that a fake unity appears in the outer shell of man until a crisis occurs to stress fragmentation at the inner core level of man.

It would appear impossible to terminate this chapter concerning the inner core of man without some mention of what has been described as one of the most important emotion man can have – love. It is said that when G-d toiled in the beginning, his work was made by love. Yet what has happened in this modern world of ours? To love was to care. We have now largely become an uncaring society, which takes rather than gives. Is it because our Wings have lost the beauty of their primitive shape, due to the production of too many instruments which have weighed them down under its burden? Or has the shape of love itself become misshapen? To love means to suffer pain and to recognize the poetry and beauty of its shape and purpose. We seem to flinch from the pain and deny the poetry and beauty of its concept and simply want the feeling of well-being which eludes us.

Love appears to be lifelike, it expands and contracts according to the stimuli injected into it. Love also has a shape, but that shape is capable of changing into many combinations when it relates to the relationship between man and woman. Ideally, one person should have achieved oneness with his or her physical and spiritual consciousness swell as with communication with G-d. Ideally, when that oneness enters another oneness it becomes an un-fragmented entity of oneness. The shape of this is like a dot within a circle represented by waves outside the circle. The dot and the circle represent the oneness of man and woman, both able to contract and expand, the dot into the circle and the circle into the dot. Both revolving around the same axis. When two people arrive at this state of oneness, G-d's presence is always there and becomes part of the circle and of the dot. But when oneness is fragmented, then one becomes two and separation occurs further and further. It then seems that there is a multiplicity of combinations, because with two separate entities one can be two, three or four and the chance of one entity being able to enter an entity that has fragmented and then arrive at the ideal oneness is remote. It is in this situation when love loses its poetry, beauty and soul consciousness and becomes purely physical or purely spiritual that the Wings have lost their lustre and have become clipped due to the pain and the joy becoming unhinged. The shape of love does not necessarily have to be represented by a circle but can adapt its own original shape to that of an oblong, square, rectangle or triangle providing it maintains the same axis or hinge so that the centre of gravity remains unchanged.

If the shape is fragmented then it becomes more difficult to associate and unite genuinely with another or becomes lost in the waves of the world that encircles the shape. Also, G-d cannot easily enter a fragmented shape with the same power because there exists many poles of gravity all with various attractions which become disorientated rather than coordinated, even in the movement of life, with contraction that cannot flourish, and expansion never ending and unable to find a balance.

Providing it is accepted that love can take the form of many shapes and that the axis or hinge can remain constant, then there can be no such thing as racialism because the colour of a man or woman's skin is irrelevant.

In the world today shapes are being more and more fragmented in human relationships. As a result, the family unit, the mainstay of our society, is beginning to crumble. This also applies to nations who have all taken different shapes unable to bond on the same hinge or axis. It follows that there can be no real alliances between them until they adapt their shape to fit in the same hinge or axis.

All these nations are so engrossed in consuming from their own resources and others, regardless of their structure, that they have forgotten they are part of the five continents that make up the world and the five lines of gravity that direct the world, in the same way as the five muscular chains direct the life line of man.

Chapter XI
THE SPIRIT OF MAN

The spirit of man is within his own structure. Without it the structure would not be complete. Yet the spirit has a shape. It can be read from the expression of the face and the body, but still there is a distinction between a smile and a smile, tears and tears. There is a smile of circumstance, a smile to hide pain, a political smile and then there is the genuine smile which comes from the depth of one's being; the smile produced by a person contemplating a baby or that of expressing happiness at the meeting of someone held in esteem.

Tears are also a projection of the spirit and normally portray sadness or deeply felt happiness. Yet, tears can be produced at will by actors through simulation. Laughter is the essence of man and a computer would find it impossible to distinguish laughter coming from the spirit of man and laughter originating from his physical consciousness. In fact, even men find it difficult to distinguish between the two sources of laughter and this is what keeps the spirit independent from the flesh. If our reactions and the expression of our emotions stemmed only from simple physical stimuli we would be simply a biochemical structure. If we reacted only through reason we would be automatons. This is a concept that man finds difficult to fathom, that his spirit is part of his structure yet retains a life of its own. Further, everything that appears as human artefacts reflects the spirit of man. This has been seen in the instruments and tools and extends even into the spirit of laws, the spirit of fashion, the spirit of politics, economics and games. These artifacts reflect numerous facets which give shape to the spirit.

In the case of law, the spirit is involved when a particular law is originally created, how it is interpreted and in the way it is administered or enforced. In fashion the spirit is that of an original designer and reflects through the final design and fabric texture; in politics according to the policies and the way they are presented. In economics according to the direction in which they are applied. The spirit devises how they should be played or conducted. Thus, there is nothing that man does either wrongly or rightly without the original involvement of the spirit in some way.

In the same way natural phenomena represent the multiple aspects of the G-dly spirit, all creation is part of the spiritual structure. A good example is the creation of the moon and the sun which clearly reflect two opposite and complementary dimensions, each one regulating one facet of time. G-dly spirit is to be found even down to the creation of man himself bestowed with a spirit of his own that gives him a free choice. A projection of this G-dly spirit is still part of the texture that makes spirit of man free of restrictions.

The same reflection of creative spirit is also clearly displayed in art, music, literature and all other activities where man has harnessed his spirit to portray that which lies within his creative prowess, stemming from the similar source that created the moon and the sun.

The reflection can be either one of joy or of sadness producing tears from the visual aspect of a painting, from the sound of music and by reading the written word. This can touch the spiritual sensitivity of man and momentarily produce tears and ecstasy. It can also apply in a different sense when the physical and spiritual combine, for instance the creation of intense grief or anguish in death or through some act or action that is visual or an experience which man feels rather than sees.

Humour can be either expressed by speech or by mime, it can be funny in itself or because of pathos. A clown combines all these aspects to create humour and laughter in the way he dresses, acts, mimes, behaves and talks. This communication is true body language in action. It also involves the spirit of man.

Humour not only reflects the spirit of individual nations and races and the people within such nations and races, but also reflects their character and personality. It could be said that the spirit is closely aligned to personality and character and reflect its form and shape.

Language has been accepted as man's most sophisticated instrument of communication. Every language has formed its own unique sense of humour which cannot effectively be translated into another language because it strikes different chords of the spirit. In communication, the normal expectation is that there will be a response at all times. However, there are periods when the spirit requires recharging in a similar way to the body needing rest. During this period a void is created and response does not occur in articulated language. A silence is felt which usually provokes a reaction from the other party, e.g., "A penny for your thoughts", or "Hi! Are you still with us?" When there is still no reaction the person generally considers that something is wrong and tries, by any means, to signal, either by the flapping of hands, clapping, shouting to make the other person feel their presence, as if they felt that the spirit has left the person's body and because of the silence, conclude that some form of illness has struck their companion. Of course, the spirit has not left the body but is simply resting, although it does appear to irradiate life in the expected usual manner. This particular occurrence exemplifies the independent life of the spirit. It can be felt by its absence, it lives and follows the shape of the physical structure of man, it has its own entity. But the alarm bell rings when this entity seems to drift away from the physical body.

The problem is that many people are not aware of its separate status because a state of symbiosis co-exists at most times. When people realise it, they tend to live their life from one pole and are not aware that the physical has developed a dimension of its own that cannot bypass the spiritual dimension. When life is guided by the other physical pole, it becomes solely concerned with the material plane but the void of the bypassed spiritual pole is also felt. This is the case of our consumer society which appears as powerful but is full of internal conflict because it does not come into terms with the spiritual plane. Man, either knowingly or unknowingly is in daily conflict between his flesh and his spiritual consciousness. At the beginning of the twentieth century, it would appear that in many people the physical is gradually overpowering the spiritual and the danger of the created void has already left a lot of wounds open for us to ponder. Yet, we are insensitive to them because the physical entity has almost taken over completely as man descends into the realm of a non-entity where neither instinct nor reason predominates.

The truth of the matter is that the spirit of man is the most beautiful, mystical and wonderful aspect of his creation. It is breathed into him when the entity stirs with life in a mother's womb and only leaves him at death. It is indestructible and eternal and can be possessed by no one except himself. If only man realized how precious his spirit was, how it can be moulded by its own dictates, he would guard it jealously. It is a gem, a unique gift from his Creator regulating his own record of life.

The spirit of a man is that which lives even after love is dead. Because the spirit has to be refined and allowed to spiral upwards in enlightenment and knowledge during many lifetimes of experiences both good and bad, man has to treasure it and allow his physical existence to refine his spirit or soul still further. There is no other purpose and only soul consciousness can allow the process to begin. It was called by the prophets of old "to be reborn" which means to be reborn from the physical to the spiritual. In this way and from this new start man may select all his instruments and transform them so that they fit into the clearly defined triangular shape that allows him to escape from the darkness of ignorance into the light of knowledge.

All scientific discovery, philosophy and art come in the first instance from the spirit of man. It is in the soul that the germ is sown, fertilized and developed. When a baby is born it takes on the physical resemblance of its parents, but its spirit is its own – that which has been born before and lived through many lifetimes to live again so that the lesson can be learned well. Environment and surroundings will play some part in developing the entity's personality and character, but the soul remains its own possession and is neither the mother's nor the father's whose only achievement is to produce the vehicle in which the soul will reside.

It also would be true to say that all of us are in different stages of spiritual development. Some people's development is retarded by their own actions, others progress more rapidly. This is what causes turmoil and strife in the world, the continuing conflict between the spiritual and the physical, but in the end because of the very nature of creation, the physical has to be balanced with the spiritual. And, because all the spirit is part of the cosmos, its immeasurable power, energy and vitality can and does shape the destiny of man. But G-d's will ultimately has to predominate and no matter what man does, he will have to fulfil his fate on this physical plane – the true acknowledgement and refinement of his soul which in the beginning was created in the likeness of G-d.

G-d gave man ten commandments as a guideline to maintain His spirit on earth. How far have we applied these laws to our daily lives? Overall, the first five commandments refer to the relationship between G-d and ourselves and, therefore, are focused towards our spirit. Most people have largely disregarded the purpose of these commandments and have replaced them by their own set of rules, which suits their desire to live, not according to the spirit, but according to their physical and material needs.

Following this pattern, most people only consider the last five commandments to be important since they refer to the relationship between man and man rather than between man and G-d. Yet even some of these have been diluted or disregarded since they too impose restrictions on man's behaviour.

G-d's name is used in the Oath of Allegiance and in the swearing of the truth in the law courts. This has become an official procedure which has erased and held G-d not in the high position of esteem, but has reduced G-d to a symbol rather than an Infinite Power. This is in contravention of the spirit of the third commandment, this commandment being:

"Thou shalt not take the name of the Lord thy G-d in vain; for the Lord will not hold him guiltless that taketh his name in vain." It is thereby implied that one must not make a material or physical object of G-d, even by giving it the shape of a sound. G-d must remain within the spirit or soul of man as precious and must not be allowed to enter his physical consciousness i.e., the use of the name of G-d as an exclamation or even as an oath. The concept of G-d is exclusive.

Throughout the Bible, the spirit and the physical are mentioned as two separate entities dwelling in different abodes yet being unable to live without each other. In a way they are the "YIN" and "YANG" of the Tao symbol of acupuncture and Hindu religion, which are at the same time opposed and complementary. The existence of these two entities does not only come out solely in the Ten Commandments, but throughout the Old and New Testaments, particularly when prophets and saints refer to visions and dreams involving imagery.

Let us consider Daniel 2:31-37, 7:7-14, Micah 4:13 and John 13:-5, 6, 7.

Throughout these particular chapters reference is made to various animals that have wings, horns, teeth or ribs. All these parts of the animals are of triangular shape. Sometimes they fall off, sometimes they are being consumed, sometimes they appear to grow larger or increase in number; often it seems that a dramatic climax is achieved when ribs are being eaten, when a wing falls off or when a horn is being destroyed. Clearly these symbols appear as a part of the spirit which is being utterly destroyed, since the spirit appears as an ultimate triangle, as the most sophisticated articulation of the human mind, so in a literal interpretation the falling off of these objects or parts appears as the falling off of kingdoms, but in fact seems to refer to the falling off of the spirit of kingdoms. On the other hand, happiness is achieved when a little horn appears to break down all these kingdoms which have been polluted in one way or another, and instil into them a new spiritual life which will renew at the same time the physical appearance and will alter it since both are linked. Therefore, in the final analysis, there is an eternal renewal of the spirit from a little ferment of truth, whose destruction is a creative destruction as in the cycle of nature that we have previously analysed.

Although throughout the centuries man has tried to separate the spirit from the body, they cannot be divorced. This was demonstrated in 1905 by Einstein with his Theory of Relativity in which he established an equivalence between mass and matter, which was discovered many centuries earlier by Tao. All energies are linked, they travel through our body, throughout our spirit. Their physical aspect is different but they are one and are regulated by a simple principle which removes all apparent contradiction giving a synthesis of the negative and the positive, the true and the false, male and female, man and sky, man and earth. Man being both a citizen of Heaven and a citizen of Earth. Therefore, nothing is lost, nothing is gained, but all is transformed.

Chapter XII
The Shape of Woman

When considering the shape of woman there always seems to be a cloak of mystery surrounding her. In the past and nowadays in some cultures, a woman was/is shrouded with clothes to conceal her shape. Is this because man fears to see the origin of life in front of his eyes or is the sight of life too dazzling for him?

The shape of a woman is like an open-ended triangle, with her two breasts and vagina: the giving of life from the womb and the sustaining of life from the breasts. The life force coming through both ends of the triangle. She, like a man, also has two Wings. Is it that man fears that when he enters the naked open-ended triangle, the triangle will become closed and the Wings fold around him in an embrace from whence there is no escape? In truth this is what happens when a child is conceived, he is caught in the triangle of reproduction. The triangle closes and he is caught in the creative structure of the life-giving force, woman.

The shape of woman consists of Mother Earth, water and air; she is three-dimensional, whereas man is only two-dimensional, the seed represented by fire and air. The man's fire and air produce the seed which fertilizes in Mother Earth and is sustained and grows by water and air. As with the triangle, man might be frightened of the power of the earth, water and air which could, if laid bare and naked, extinguish his fire, and, therefore, make him unproductive.

The spirit of woman comes from the fertile earth, whereas the man's spirit comes from the fire that burns within him. The earth remains, whether fertile or otherwise, but the fire is fickle and is more difficult to sustain, so man must maintain dominance by shrouding life or otherwise he is always afraid to be trapped in the three-dimensional embrace that has the power to extinguish his fire. He, when going to a woman, is always a closed triangle and, therefore, he cannot absorb the woman in the same way as the woman with her open-ended triangle. Further, for the creation of woman, man gave up one of his ribs (triangles) which may develop in her beyond his expectations.

It is interesting when developing the three-dimensional theory of woman that in the Hebrew language, the word signifying woman is composed of a four-letter root (alef, yod, shin, heh) and for a man it is a three-letter root (alef, yod, shin). The letter "heh" which differentiates the word "man" from the word "woman" is the same letter which was added to "Abram" and transformed his name from "Abram" to "Abraham" thus bestowing him a life-giving force which made him a father of nations.

When considering the spiritual shape of woman, she is similar to man in that both have an open triangular shape. So it would appear that in the eyes of the Creator there is spiritually no differentiation between the sexes. G-d made man and woman in his likeness and, as they both have spiritually a similar open-ended triangular shape, it is impossible for one to absorb the other. Yet they can link together in oneness and the shape of the open-ended triangle becomes one and not two.

Both the spiritual and physical entities are either expanding through contraction or performing a movement of contraction through expansion which needs to be coordinated within these two levels in order to allow the flapping of Wings for communication and locomotion purposes. These movements could be applied to the butterfly shape, in that the two top Wings are the spiritual aspect and the two bottom Wings the physical aspect. Ideally, all Wings should flap together in oneness but there are those relationships where only the two top Wings come together and those relationships where only the bottom Wings come together. Other cases of abnormality display no differentiation or classification between any of the Wings.

All women and all men are unique one to the other and are fitted with as many Wings as required according to their degree of complexity. In some, the instinct of survival is backed by more Wings than in others, the same applies to the Wings of destruction, creativity etc.

The principal difference between man and woman lies in the antennae of life, in that woman has a deep-rooted respect for life, whereas man does not have the same instinct, since he has not physically experienced the pain of childbirth. In this respect he is not acquainted with the body language expressed through the pain and suffering of giving life.

However, with the introduction of sophisticated birth control methods, all women now have the choice of closing up the life-giving triangle of their physical shape, so becoming like a man with the same possibilities of a man. As a result of this, man is expected to have lost his fear of being absorbed by woman's life-giving triangle and is bewildered in his movement. The introduction of this new instrument is double-bladed: it has removed fear but has created another void, the need of being Winged and taken into the original embrace.

Woman's physical triangle is no longer open and her Wings no longer automatically close in a life-giving embrace. She desires to experience the new-found freedom of experimentation of other movements, feels herself liberated from man's closed triangular embrace, and feels free to fly wherever her Wings and antennae take her. Man, in his confusion, encourages the flight, thinking it is for his own physical well-being and, in doing so, he loses his dominance and dampens his spiritual fire.

Due to the Winged flight of many emancipated women, the child loses the joy, warmth and comfort of the Wings that used to shield him and, because the three elements of air, water and fire have lost their power, becomes fragmented as the overall design of the structure collapses.

Man in his desire to possess woman both body and soul without understanding the truth of her entity, has brought this upon himself because he could not face the dazzling, naked truth of the life-giving force – the woman whose original purpose was not to absorb him but to share his spiritual rhythmic fire and give life back to him in exchange for life.

Because of this ignorance of the shape of woman, the spiritual shape is being distorted and a warp in social structure is appearing that destroys true union and leads to fragmentation and ultimate destruction from within. This is akin to a renegade cell entering a structure which already had some weakness so that the natural antibodies do not resist and give way to the revolution that entered it until total annihilation occurs.

Chapter XIII
THE INSTRUMENT OF THOUGHT AND SPEECH

It has been accepted by modern linguists concerned with the science of linguistics that there is no link at all between the shape and sound of words and their actual meaning. Throughout this study we have seen how far the visual shape and the shape of sound influence movement and meaning of each artefact and non-artefact including man himself. Why should there be an exception with languages, another instrument of man which inspires greatly his movement and meaning?

When a baby is born, he is not yet considered complete until he has been given a name. Parents generally give a lot of thought before shaping a sound, which will be associated to the body and spirit of this new entity. They give the impression and they feel from their inner self that the sound they choose, will play a great influence in their child's destiny and will somehow alter his/her movement in the cycle of life. The name will not be meaningless and, although most forenames have lost their original meaning through use, they have not been chosen by chance but because their particular shape and sound convey a meaning which can only be expressed through subjectivity rather than through well-articulated reason.

Some writers have noticed that there is definitely some sort of linkage both in the character and destiny of people with the same forename. Although they try to stress the importance conveyed by the intrinsic meaning of various names, most people have not given this matter much thought.

In order to stress how far the name definitely changes direction of human entities by giving them a will of their own, adding another dimension again and giving them full existence, we shall still require the reader to glance at his Bible and particularly the story of Abraham and Sarah. Originally Abraham was called Abram and Sarah was called Sarai, until G-d changed their names to Abraham and Sarah. There had to be a reason for this change so let us consider what this reason might be.

Abraham was the first man who put his energies towards G-d rather than towards man and this sacrifice gave him another dimension and he became the first human being in his own right. The change of name corresponded to a change in his structure and by adding one letter (heh), He added a new dimension to his being.

So let us consider the letter "heh" both in its written form and its sound shape. In its written form, it is composed of one character within another (ה) but they are separated from each other, and it seems that the larger character is embracing the smaller one as if protecting it by its Wing. It can be interpreted as the two separate entities of man, i.e., the body living attached to the soul and protecting it by its shell. In between, the path of life is open at both ends, leaving man free choice. As far as the shape of the sound is concerned, the "heh" sounds like a gush of air coming through an "h" as if the soul which was originally blown into the nostrils of man when he was first formed, is taking a more precise shape. There seems to be no chance in the addition of this particular letter to the name of this Patriarch.

Let us now consider the transformation of Sarai to Sarah. Although it seems that there was no addition of an extra letter, but simply a transformation from one letter to another, we can still foresee some evincing design. In her original name the yod which is made out of one single character was transformed into the heh i.e., the same added letter as in Abraham. So that the letter composed of one character is transformed into a letter composed of two characters. The possible interpretation of which we have seen above. The primitivism of sterility of one single character is transformed into a structure composed of two elements. As far as the sound is concerned, the yod is read as "ai", it is a diphthong made up of two linked vowels, the sequence of which is an "a" followed by "i". In France and in French speaking countries, this sound is associated with physical pain or well-being. It is the sound of physical life. The same applies to most Arab countries where the sequence a/i applies in the onomatopoeic "ahit" also usually uttered at moments of pain and sometimes at moments of bliss. Further, in many songs, singers add the sounds "lai, lai" or "zai, zai" to music to complete the melody without words. However, one never hears the use of the sound "lia, lia" or "zia, zia" in any melody for the same purpose. It would seem then that the "i" followed by "a" refers to moral rather than physical life. This also appears in Tao' "Yin-Yang" where the vowel "i" is opposed to the vowel "a" and yet they are both connected and cling together as one. So Sarah becomes herself, a full human entity with a soul of her own. She is also awarded a new dimension which in a way will remove some of her primitive and sterile structure.

Abraham's and Sarah's problem of sterility was dealt with by chemical linguistics. By linking the two hehs together, i.e., four characters, the four Wings were united and could ensure future posterity by allowing the birth of another fully-formed human being.

A further point that should be mentioned is that two characters were added on to Abram and one character was added to Sarai. When forming a child man bears both sexes in his sperm, whereas woman only bears the one sex until the three elements are linked by the entry of the sperm into a woman's womb where the selection occurs.

The two characters added in "Abram" and fused into the one character added to Sarai, seem to shape the general pattern of genetics which is concerned only with the physiological aspect, although in this conception of creation, the two spirits must also be linked in order to achieve creation in the structure.

There are those cases of parents who long to have children but for no apparent reason the woman cannot conceive. This is not always due to any physical reason but to a mental blockage in the subconscious mind of either one or both sexes which prevents conception.

In this modern age we do not necessarily give enough thought to the spiritual aspect of conception, but simply consider the physical function of reproduction. Here again, one may wonder how many people, when giving a name to a baby, consciously or unconsciously are relating that name to a memory or an idea of some other person who may have affected their own life, a memory either in a physical sense or mentally from a book, film or other form of literature. As we are all conditioned by vibrations, is it not possible that when we give a name to a baby of such a person in our memory, we attract to the baby some form of vibration from that person and that we are keeping alive the spiritual memory of that person so that the spirit remains eternal as it returns continuously through the cycle of life?

Modern linguists do not appear to be particularly attracted by the aspect which relates to vibrations and instead concentrate on the comparison letter by letter, of words which do not appear to have any connection between shape and meaning within one language or other unrelated languages. In this study we shall concentrate instead on general aspects of language, in which the same breath of meaning seems to be involved when dealing with life, since when a language is studied, lifeguard movement cannot be divorced from such a study. In this regard, let us consider the prepositions of movement, such as "in", "on", "from" and "into". In most languages they seem to be constructed from one or two vibrations at the most. This is because when going in a particular direction, it is necessary for the sound and shape of the word to be concise. These words have short roots, and as with vibrations, they do not have more than one or two basic roots. This fact unites both related and unrelated Semitic and non-Semitic languages, so that the universal shape and sounds appear when the movement of life is at stake. After the movement, when there is more time available, the connection between languages seems to break out and words have a totally different number of vibrations.

In order to understand the reason why the vibrations differ so much in number, shape and sound, although they refer to one object which seems to be universal through the naked eye, let us examine a simple example, that of a young girl with her mother who goes to a bakery to purchase a loaf of bread and returns home. Once she steps into the home, she is steeped in a completely different atmosphere from that of the bakery and the outside world. When her mother removes the bread from her basket and lays it on the table, in the child's mind the bread is not the same bread, it has a different texture. By means of association her spirit prints into the loaf a different vibration. It is not just an ordinary loaf of bread, it is the bread from home and the same applies to all the other items that she relates in spirit to her home. The same different print in spirit, through subjective associations, applies to the fact that bread is "bread" in English, "pain" in French, "chlieb" in Russian, etc.

Although to a computer it is the same artefact, to a human being living in a different environment it is not the same one. Its shape has a particular sound and number of vibrations, because it has been transformed through the spirit. In the same way, coins are coins obtained through labour, but each task is different to obtain them and different nations have tried to project their own prints by projecting different prints onto the coins. Most have a figure on one side and a leaf, a tree or an artefact design on the other.

Where financial exchange is concerned a mathematical conversion is required which can be done by a machine as well as by the human brain. As far as linguistic exchange is concerned the computer cannot do the conversion, because the spirit of man is the only one which can possibly enter the spirit of another man.

There is no chance in the shape of words, in the print of words as minute print of coins where another aspect of linguistics is involved, that of semiotics.

Why are leaves a common feature in most coins? Is it simply because they convey the idea of multitude or is it the print of the leaf which breathes the air, consumes the water through its nervous pattern, and is very much alike in shape to that of the nervous system of man without which speech could not exist?

All the facts of life stress how far the spiritual entity influences the physical entity down to the creation of all instruments, including the instrument of language. Yet although in the spiritual sense language appears to be of the same shape, it diversifies in the physical usage of the spoken and written word from one nation to another. Is this because we only think in a two-dimensional way with just shape and meaning and eliminate the third dimension conveyed by spiritual print which seems to give a different association and shape to the word, but enhances its unity?

With regard to thought, the human being is basically only in a two-dimensional stage of development as with a child who is being weaned and does not know the difference between the intake and rejection of food or the little girl who separates the two breads. It is not until we are able to advance beyond this stage and enter three-dimensional thinking that we will express our thoughts in a universal language. The seed is there, since in a child's mind there already exists a universal grammar.

It would seem then that the human being is gradually moving towards the same thought and because of this he creates the same basic instruments in order to broaden his Wings. Language is the last instrument which seems to resist movement towards the same superficial direction and this shows clearly the false knowledge which gave birth to a lie due to a misunderstanding of the triangular shape. Although instruments can be standardized, language cannot truly recognize its soul consciousness.

We seem to create more and more Wings by producing more and more instruments of communication, locomotion etc. but, because we are not building the same instruments of thought and speech, these are not unified and, therefore, thought is not blended. This can be viewed by a comparison of the various laws in different countries concerning relationships between human beings which are basically, if not totally, made of the same breath. So if we do not have a philosophy of life based on respect, moderation and consumption and accept the oneness of our Maker we cannot let a universal language drown our spirit. Thinking in three dimensions can only give birth to unity and, therefore, to the desire to communicate universally both in shape and sound in a unified manner.

Chapter XIV
NUMBERS, LETTERS AND FIGURES

Numbers should not be considered apart from the general aspect of life. Geometrical shapes have numbers, a triangle is three, a square is four etc. Even human beings are subject to numbers, their date of birth, age and other data including size of individual parts of the body, important to medical science.

Numbers were in existence from the beginning in that Creation was based on six active pulsations plus a pulsation of rest. This does not mean literally seven days, but one definite pulsation occurring, then followed by another regardless of the time factor. Alternatively, man was created into two basic pulsations. One shaped his physical structure and the other shaped his spiritual structure. Animals on the other hand had only one pulsation when it came to their final creation.

It has been said that the whole of creation and life itself is based on numbers and letters, and that everything when reduced down to its basic shape, sound or pulsation, is no more than a mathematical formula. In spite of this basic concept, most human beings like to separate shapes from numbers as if they were two separate offsprings from the mind which in fact is only one.

In Hebrew each letter is associated to a number and the succession of numbers corresponds to the ordinary succession of letters in the alphabet. Succession is an important factor in the development of mathematics and, since all mathematics requires reasoning, it follows that numbers are linked by certain laws of logic in order to make equations. The same reasoning seems to apply to language, although modern linguistics do not conclude that the shape of words and their sounds are linked in a similar meaningful approach. In biblical Hebrew there seems to be a profound meaning in the way letters are put together and numerology explains why some letters appear a certain number of times compared to others. For example, the word used in the Bible meaning "to form" in the sense a human was formed by G-d contains the "yod" twice amongst other letters, whereas the word relating to the forming of animals is virtually the same but contains only one yod. This distinction between man and animal is highlighted within the word itself without any further philosophy being necessary. In fact, serious students of the Torah usually count up the total of each letter when studying a word or concept and give meaning to the word according to the total given by adding up each letter used as a number and they may even inverse each character as if re-arranging figures as in an equation. We shall not go as far as studying the Torah in the same approach, but will try to convey the connection between figures, letters and philosophy by giving some guidelines for this concept to be understood. In Hebrew there is only one letter which can be read either as a consonant or as the vowel, thus breaking the opening and closing sound barrier. It is the letter "vav" which looks like a wand and its numerical value is six.

We have five fingers in our hand plus an antenna which guides them so that the figure six appears as a hinge connecting two different worlds, spirit and body. As a consonant the "vav" is pronounced as "v", as a vowel it is pronounced either as "o" as in "know" or "u" as in "rule" according to the word which one must know in advance.

In Hebrew grammar it transforms the past into future and the future into past. The whole philosophy based on the notion of time depends on the little nothing on the letter, on the sound, on a figure, on the lack of classification. The most holy name of G-d contains this letter as well as the letter yod. It also contains the "heh" twice, which we have seen in "Abraham" and "Sarah" so that no chance seems to appear in such a formation of the name of G-d himself. The total number of letter values in this holy name of G-d, which must not be pronounced out of deep respect, is 26.

"Aleph", the first letter of the Hebrew alphabet, has therefore the figure "one" as its numerical value. It corresponds to "a", the first letter of the English and French alphabet and many languages. Its body is made out of two yods which look like little embryos, geometrically divided and opposed by a "vav" which looks like a wand. By adding up, the number "26" is also obtained. This figure corresponds to the figure "eight" when adding up two and six. Eight is the figure representing miracle over normality in the Judaic philosophy. It is not by chance that circumcision of newly born males must normally be carried out on the eighth day? There are seven days in the week and after the seventh day, it is the figure eight which brings us to the world of the eighth day of resurrection of endless continuity of eternal alliance with our Maker. All beginnings including the first letter of an alphabet contain some seed of eternity. The whole philosophy brought into being is stressed by the body structure and corresponding figures of the letter "a" whose numerical value is one, but which can germinate into eight, unity and eternity are not separated from the very beginning.

Let us take the second letter of the Hebrew alphabet, it is a consonant which has two names "bet" and "vet" because it can be read either as "b" or "v". It looks like a cell which is opening up. Its figure is "two". Since it can also be pronounced as "v" as the "Vav", it may therefore be linked to the figures one and eight. In fact, the "Vav" is one of the essential components that make up the "aleph" and the holy name of G-d previously mentioned. Two is the figure of duality, man and woman, body and spirit, negative and positive, all living as one through the eternal cycle of life, so that the figure "two" cannot be dissociated from the entire cosmos.

Another letter which displays the two alternate sound characteristic, still in the Hebrew alphabet, is the letter which corresponds to the French and English "f" because it is sometimes pronounced "p" and sometimes "ph". Is it not surprising that the French and English "ph" is also pronounced "ph" as in 'philosophy'? The first commandment to man after his creation was "be fruitful and multiply" which is linked an eternal cycle of life.

Beyond the meaningfulness of individual letters corresponding to figures, let us consider a full word by adding up all its letters, in particular the word meaning "life" in Hebrew which is pronounced "hai". By adding up the two letters of this word, i.e., "het" (eight) and "yod" (10), we obtain the number 18 which can be reduced down to nine, which one finds again without fail by adding up its multiples 18, 27, 36 etc. so that the infinitely calculated reproduction is given to us in the 8 (of 18) that mirrors eternity to the ten fingers of our hand (letter "yod"/10) which indicates that eternity is within the grasp of a man's hand.

It remains to analyse the figure seven since there are seven pulsations in the creation of the world. The word "hand" is pronounced "yad" in Hebrew (Yod, Dalet). Yod equals ten, "d" which is the name of Dalet equals four, so by adding up ten and four, fourteen is obtained and by dividing by two, seven is obtained. So the essence of the meaning of the word "hand" is reduced down to the meaning of the number seven which constitutes the seven days of the week also regulating our lives. This in turn represents the eternity which lies in G-d's hand linked to our hands.

Another word which adapts to the number seven is the word "nothing" (zero) without which mathematics could not exist and mathematics exists from the invention or concept of 0 (zero) as well as from the concept of succession. Do we not live according to little nothings which animate or extinguish the rhythm of our lives and is it not so that there is only a little nothing between normality and abnormality? Therefore, in the relationship between letters and numbers there is also a little nothing, so that by using numbers, the full meaning of words becomes apparent; by the same token, using words produces numbers all linked to the eternal multiple of man, in both his physical and spiritual self, linked to the eternal Creation and the concept of G-d. Indeed, the human soul will never die but will always reappear, in the same way as the figure nine reappears, through its infinite multiples coming as the water stemming from everywhere including the vivid source of our tears of happiness and our tears of sorrow, both from the same eye ducts. It takes nine months and one week to give birth to a child, but most people do not recognize the significance of this, even though they are obsessed with figures especially in matters of statistics and with symbols especially in matters of religion. Nine is the multiple of three which is the figure that represents the three dimensions of man: fire, water, and air (spirit, physical and material), the three points of the philosophical triangle and all the diversity of life which conceals the oneness which stems from the figure three. Conversely, light depends upon the understanding of the figure three and therefore, on the meaning of the triangle. The human being is the only mammal which takes the longest time to become physically self-reliant. This has been scientifically observed, but the spiritual aspect of self reliance has not been placed under the microscope of science. It may have a similar pattern. Perhaps it will take longer than our stage of development for our spirit to be able to achieve the same advancement as our physical being, even though compared with many other mammals, our physical being appears puny by comparison and it is only with the power which lies within man's soul that he is able to remain dominant. Yet psychic phenomena are not considered for any illnesses in modern societies. They are only commercially used for thrillers.

The psychology of numbers has not yet been properly explained and researched. The fact is, they have a far greater philosophical and psychological significance than most people realize, for instance in music, whether it be pop or classical, there is an underlying melody which can be reduced to a number, such a number can signify attraction or repulsion to a particular individual and in this way it can be analysed by the sequence of numbers within the melody, e.g., if the number is five, it may signify particular importance given to the five meridians regulating our life. If it is nine it may signify the eternal reproduction of the species. If it is three, it focuses on the three-dimensional man. The reason why there could exist attraction and repulsion is that it spiritually either detracts or expands from the core of the soul. It is possible to analyse the evolution of man by pinpointing the evolution of different links of attraction of music reduced to numbers. This is particularly so in national anthems because by numbers and step by step counting down the pulsation of the words that stick to music it displays the history of a nation and to which aspect its spirit is evolving.

We will take for example the French National anthem, the Marseillaise, and analyse it down to numbers, based on the principles described above. We will then compare it with the British national anthem to discover the difference if any in the spiritual aspirations of both nations. The Marseillaise in the method that has been adopted displays the following figures: 10, 8, 9, 8, 8, 9, 8, 7, 10, 6, 6, 2, 2, 4, 6.

10 represents the Ten Commandments regulating spiritual life. It can also be seen as a multiple of the original five regulating the five muscular chains.

8 represents a miracle beyond normality.

9 represents reproduction.

7 represents repetition of time through the regular pattern

of seven days of the week and the seven pulsations of the Creation of the world.

6 is the multiple of the original three which is unity through the triangle and represents the three dimensions.

2 is the binary relation which reflects the two poles of opposed attractions connected together in order to live.

4 represents half way through eternity because eight is a multiple, so in a way it contains the seeds of eternity.

It will be noticed that in the sequence of numbers, eight is followed by eight which gives a total of sixteen. In order to understand the meaning of the figure we must return to the butterfly shape.

Basically, the four Wings represent four triangles attached to two hinges, a top hinge and a bottom hinge. Each Wing represents three which multiplied by four gives the figure twelve plus two hinges and two antennae gives the figure sixteen. The prime number of sixteen is two. Two is man's dilemma of the two poles of attraction, physical and spiritual, positive and negative, the masculine and feminine dimension, which he separates rather than links together. The words of the Marseillaise e.g., "L'étendard sanglant est levé" (the flag full of blood is drawn up) portrays the physical suffering of man to achieve physical and spiritual unity. The impression given is that both are rising upwards out of their structure to achieve an awakening.

It will also be noticed that there are two sixes following each other. This gives the figure 12, which is a multiple of which is 3. The figure three represents the triangle and the Wing, and projects the four Wings of the butterfly which come into birth through the twelve tribes, where each tribe was assigned a particular task which was to improve the overall creation of G-d.

So that if the butterfly appears as the mechanical instrument of G-d, there is need for a spiritual instrument which can be given through the figure ten of the Ten

Commandments added to the butterfly figure. In this way we obtain the figure twenty-six, which as we have seen is one of the figures of the name of G-d.

The grand total of this anthem is 103 which is unity, nothing and three dimensions, which might be interpreted as a little nothing hiding the unity of the three dimensions. When added up, this figure can be reduced to four which is half way through miracle over normality that can be achieved when the triangle is fully understood and man stops misinterpreting unity and oneness.

When singing an anthem or melody which has a refrain, sometimes the memory fades away at a certain stage so that some words which stick to the music might be forgotten. However, the numbers that correspond to the beat of the music are never forgotten, as if numbers appear to be strongly imprinted in the memory far easier and more safely than words, so that the core of the message cannot be forgotten.

With regard to the British anthem, the same concept of the numbers is given as for the French National anthem. By adopting the same method the following figures are given: 6, 6, 4, 6, 6, 6, 5.

Six is the predominant figure, which is the multiple of the original three which is unity through the triangle.

Four represents half way through eternity.

Five is the number regulating the five muscular chains representing the link between the two aspects of man.

If the five sixes are added up the number 30 is obtained. Since three represents the triangle and zero represents conception, it would appear that Britain has been conceived through the triangle or been blessed with it. If all the figures are added, the number 39 is obtained, and if you add three and nine, you obtain the number 12, which represents the four Wings of the butterfly. If thirty-nine is divided by three you obtain the number 13 which could represent the thirteenth lost tribe of Israel. It has been suggested that this may be the tribe of David and there seems to be an amazing link between this national anthem and the name David. In the Hebrew the numerical value of David is 4. 6. 4 and the national anthem solely uses these figures apart from a 5.

So far it has been thought that the Hebrew is the sole language able to manipulate numbers to represent theories. This analysis shows that this is applicable to almost any language when the words are connected to music. The above analysis, based on Kabbalah, the Jewish oral tradition of mystical interpretation of the Old Testament, shows that this theory is not solely restricted to learned Kabbalists, but to anyone willing to decode the secret of any mystical message conveyed through poetry or music.

Chapter XV
Classification

Prior to the Industrial Revolution when there was a quickening in science and technology, man classified each thing or object according to its appearance, shape and size. Since then there has been a trend to declassify and over-classify or not classify at all, until there appeared some confusion, leading to destruction. Man has developed so many instruments that he no longer knows exactly what he has created. Then, by consuming spiritual and physical knowledge without classification, the antennae have been unable to direct the Wings in any particular direction. In this respect we will deal first with the environment. This involves the three natural dimensions of the triangle from which man was created, since he came from earth and since earth cannot be prolific without two other elements – air and water. Since the three elements are at the base of his environment, man in his short sightedness has failed to link these three elements and considers each element as one separate entity and from each element tries to classify each and every aspect of this single dimension. So, instead of having a triangle we have three separate wands which are scattered without unification and each dimension then branches off into a fragmented void.

In the beginning there were seven pulsations for the creation of different elements composing the world. Each element stemming from a shapeless form. When each element took shape it was to be distinguished from the other, water from earth etc. Each had its set allocated positions that shape meant distinction, which meant classification down to the smallest element composing the overall structure. Therefore, because of classification and variety, unity is hidden nowadays and man's media focuses on a clutter of images and sounds which can even appeal to our touch and depict so closely to life a drop of rain that can be heard, seen and felt, that man finds it difficult to differentiate between the natural and the man-made object.

Let us focus on the creation of animals that were formed from the earth and from a triangle stemming from a first "yod" (10) in the first stage. When man who was created after them gave each one a name, he created a bond with them by language, his most sophisticated instrument. And, by giving them a name according to their inner mission that appealed to man, man shaped destiny over them ("dominion over them").

Man was fitted with "yod" as his animal counterpart. His spiritual fire came at a second stage (second "yods") by a pulsation of air though his nostrils. This pulsation enabled language to become part of man's spiritual triangle. When woman appeared from man's "rib" (overall triangle), she also acquired one "yod "(earth – physical triangle) and another "yod" (heaven- spiritual triangle).

All these living creatures lived in a garden environment and were told to consume all fruit except for one. At this stage, they were told to distinguish products that could be consumed and others that should be rejected, but the distinction was not clearly explained. Man did not wish to be told about selection without understanding fully the root of the danger and to refrain from "touching" a lie that crumbled the truth. This is one product through a mere telepathic order was not enough – as he had a desire to develop a reason of his own. From this decision followed the removal of this direct telepathic communication with G-d, of his third eye, which gave him the vision of G-d's messengers and of the aura. He thus became naked, deprived of all these original arrays and extra spiritual Wings that gave him a natural vision of differentiating creation from destruction, fertility from sterility, ecology from pollution, communication from nuclear warfare. His physical nakedness or consciousness in having lost his Wings followed the general movement in the same manner as limbs follow the head when a baby leaves his mother's womb. Once man lost his protective shell and since nature does not like a void, it was eventually replaced by another kind of shell – the Ten Commandments – the body and texture of the Torah. This gave to mankind the concept of the sanctity of human life and the dignity of every human being. So this written way of life was no longer based on instinct and yet it stemmed from the original command of consuming all fruit, except one.

We have already analysed the commandments and seen how far they appeal to making a choice through selection of the one G-d, respect for His creation and rejecting the mixing of seeds of different kinds. As man had more and more Wings removed and replaced by reason and respect, more and more dilution occurred, as far as putting into practice the given knowledge is concerned, in the same way as a child does not like to be told that fire burns until he painfully feels what it means. However, in spite of rejection, more and more guidelines were added to the Torah and gave it a denser aspect but because man had become "naked" he divided his physical tissular reason from his spiritual reason so that even nowadays he is blurred in his choices.

Pollution of the air, the earth and the water occurs due to man's descent into his physical consciousness and because of this his naked spirit is starved and his imaginary physical needs create overconsumption, easy rejection and an uncaring attitude towards nature. Man, due to this denial of his spirit, is creating for himself a void caused by destruction of the environment. This stems through man's original rejection of his three extra spiritual senses (telepathy, third eye and direct communication with G-d) which he replaces with consumption, without classification, regardless of origin as if these original endowments could be replaced with his own hands. By letting his structure be entered by anything at any time, the overall product cannot be digested, so that parts will be naturally evacuated while other waste products will still remain within him, poisoning him and making it easy for any form of cancer to spread within his's structure and, since man is part of the whole chain of nature, he will spread his own illness and contaminate water, air and fire.

Perhaps the worst element in man is his destructive capability which seems to be inbred in his tissular memory, both physically and spiritually. This probably stemmed from his rejection of the third eye, direct communication with G-d and his resentment at the loss of protection that followed this rejection. He found himself left to his own resources without guidance and then proceeded to over-consume and reject thoughtlessly that which he failed to classify in the beginning, resulting in destruction of himself and the environment in which he lives. He tends to separate himself into creativeness and destruction, therefore, in simple terms, he will build then recklessly destroy that which he has created. He creates beauty and ugliness with the same instruments without differentiation or classification and with the passing of time his resentment and, therefore, destructiveness, increase due to his lack of understanding of the laws which govern his behaviour and nature.

Man has an inbred fascination to kill and destroy himself by the use of destructive instruments (weapons). This has existed throughout the generations, until he now has the capacity not only to destroy himself, but the entire planet on which he lives. This destructiveness is due to his misinterpretation of and attraction to the triangular shape; when a man speaks to another man he is attracted by the other man's triangle that appears in his face, in the movement of his arms forming angles, without consideration of the other side of man, which is made of a circular shape and yet man is made with triangles (face) etc. and circles (skull) and cells. The circle cannot be misinterpreted since it does not produce angles but only rolls on following the law of gravity whereas the triangle tries to go against it. Most ball games lead to a concentration of men or women; they gather crowds towards one centre of attraction rather than scatter them as do the triangular instruments created by man. An exception to it seems to be the cannon ball, but because its base is made out of a triangle, the circle is overridden by the triangle. Man seems to have gone so far in his destructive impulses that nowadays even ball games have a final destructive aim because the triangle of money has entered the circle of life.

One could explain this destructive image further by reminding the reader of the birth of a child who screws up his hands into a circle as soon as he is born and, when he grows bigger, screws up and tears any paper given to him until the paper is destroyed. When a man dies he does not clutch any more, but opens up his palms as if he tries to signify that it took him a lifetime to dominate his destructive impulse of possession.

When reducing classification down to geometrical shapes it appears that there are three basic possibilities. First the wands may pursue an outwards movement so that life of the three elements will never meet up. Second, it may be an inward movement so that there may be some connections achieved, although the connecting point would be within two poles of attraction without a real link. The third possibility will require a strenuous effort from all elements to achieve a torsion so that when the inward movement occurs, the final connection will focus on to one single pole, which will give a unique philosophy of life-based infertility and sanctity of vegetable, animal and human life. Since man has stemmed from earth, in the same way as a vegetable seed, he would choke if he was reverting down to earth, since air would be missing although he would have enough water. For his physical survival man has realized that he cannot revert back into the earth, but also needs the air. Perhaps sometime he will realize the importance of fire beyond this physical realization in order to expand his soul consciousness.

Man's lack of classification leads to the reckless utilization of the vital raw resources of the world without any consideration being given as to their replacement. Raw materials extracted from the earth evolve slowly through evolution and take countless generations to be replaced if this is possible. Yet man seems to live for the present and does not take into his reckoning the needs and requirements of future generations. This also extends to the species of animals. If these can be used for either food or some other by-products, man will carry on destroying without restraint nor classification until the species become extinct. The triangle of his environment is not recognized and he lives in a cloud of confusion due to his obsession with separation that has shadowed unity. This compulsion leading to separation has taken him to such an extent that it has led him to become dismantled. His top Wings are now hinged in the lower hinge and vice versa. His two antennae are still there, but cannot guide the structure anymore because the centre of gravity has been lost, However, on the outside the butterfly shape appears as a constant feature, the original movement of flying cannot be performed.

Instead of concentrating on correctly assembling his own shape, men preferred to focus on assembling the pieces of an airplane in order to fly, since his own structure could not allow him to fly. Although he can fly with the help of this instrument, external to his structure, therein still no direction or purpose and the antennae still cannot guide the flying instrument. The plane is still waiting to be guided and, although the system looks very sophisticated with airport controllers guiding the pilot through radars and other instruments, the movement is not self-contained, but is expanding endlessly.

Classification

Due to the over-creation of instruments aiming at higher and higher power, there has been a breakdown in real communication in this century, even though it has been described as a century of communication. This is a continuation of the Tower of Babel which led to a diversity of languages, through man wanting to display his powerful Wings. The tower today could be the micro-chip and the computer, whereby man is still unconsciously endeavouring to prove his might and superiority to his Creator. He travels to the moon, yet cannot adequately talk to his next door neighbour. He tries to understand the language of the extra-territorial beings haunting his imagination, but cannot understand his own language or his problem stemming from a lack of classification and understanding of the Bible that he has reduced down to mechanical performances where the spiritual fire is absent. At this level we have rejected through consumption as in the child who was being weaned and was unaware of the difference between the inward and outward movement because his tissular memory was not yet formed to inoculate him with a "natural" sense of distinction.

The world was created from a void which led to certain shapes. Now the possibility is twofold: either reverting to another void which does not look void because of the movements and shapes distracting us or going to a world composed of fully structured shapes, which allows us to fly with our own Wings without the compulsive need of superficial instruments, in the hope that our antennae will at last find their original purpose.

The overall hope that our antennae will find the original fire that guided them depends on the instrument of our hands, on the number five and the careful selection of instruments that will allow expansion of our spiritual and physical coordinated movements.

Chapter XVI
Politics

Politics, ideally, is man's conception to maintain and administer his instrument of an organized social structure and should revolve around the pole of one ethic of life. In fact, unfortunately, it has fragmented around an increasing number of poles to the detriment of man. Due to his lack of classification, which has broken down his structure, politics deals with different aspects of his damaged elements without considering the overall structure. Politicians try to reshape one Wing, one antenna, and consider themselves as physicians specializing in one particular field of research. However, as medical specialists of non-energetic medicine, they maintain an emprise over man with arguments which appear and sound logical but blur man from his own direction rather than repair his Wings, hinges and antennae. Various completely opposed poles of ethics assail man's structure in order to fragment it further and further.

Because of a division in the world of politics, it has appeared that a greater division was necessary in order to maintain power, leading to even more fragmentation of each element of the individual. In order to conceal this division, concentration of political ideologies of various origins and often opposite aims and purpose create a shapeless form, giving the impression that it has a base fully structured with shape and content. This is achieved by the help of man's media and advertising, emphasizing charisma, external appeal and appearance and considering as a secondary importance the basic movement of life, which is often unknown to the political instrument.

In order to appeal, politics and politicians have realized the need of building up a structure so that their credibility can be established. This structure contains some elements that refer to some human elements. Political parties are often referred to as "bodies" and generally labelled as left Wing and right Wing.

Politics can be even further compared to man since each element shaping it can also be fitted into the butterfly shape. The two antennae represent the left and right political philosophies, the two top Wings represent the government and the ruling party hinged together by the executive and administration, the two bottom Wings represent labour and business hinged together by the trade unions and business institutions. The butterfly shape, although it appears structured, is in fact separated by its inability to coordinate its various individual structures together. Each country's basic butterfly structure is the same, but the ailment varies in its degree of coordination and separation. This situation reflects on its links with other countries which can also be disjointed.

Due to this lack of coordination, man who is already dismantled, is unable to fuse together his own Wings to the Wings that are supposed to represent him and fulfil his needs. This instrument, more than any other, prevents his flight and keeps him earthbound.

The two main political philosophies can be reduced into simple terms, the left Wing wants to expand its influence into more state control over business and monopolies, whereas the right Wing contracts its control over them. Both are trying to obtain expansion, whereas in fact they more often than not achieve contraction. The movement is not coordinated and often fragmented due to the lack of communication not only with the body politic, but in its communication with labour, business and the trade unions. They lack the primitive instinct of the movement of contraction and expansion, consumption and rejection. More often than not, one political philosophy concentrates on one movement or other regardless of over-production and over-use of resources. Man is encouraged to demand more and more instruments and products surplus to his requirements, so that many more instruments are being produced and rejected. This results in man being inflated greater than he really is and, because of his imagined picture larger than human dimension, he is portrayed as a superman who needs greater and greater instruments and products in order to survive. Water is no longer a basic requirement. Instead, a man-made processed liquid of a particular make is the only answer that will quench his thirst and give him the perfect movement.

The same applies to all manufactured and processed products including food which are all still comprised of earth and water. However, these primitive elements have been forgotten in the infectious consumer spiral in which possessions are easily acquired and readily consumed, disposed of or re-acquired.

Thus, the true dimension of man is shrouded beneath a blanket of deception, so that he no longer knows the correct scale of his structure. Politics have been caught in the web of the consumer spiral and governments cannot contain it in either size or dimension since they rely totally on the popularity of the electee. Therefore, they too are contained within their own uncoordinated inflated structure and flight is becoming gradually more difficult with the antennae of political philosophy more and more imprisoned in their own inability to expand and contract to coordinate the structure. This is mainly due to each Wing and hinge expanding greater than its capacity creating a lack of harmony and balance during expansion and causing pressure on other parts and aspects of its overall structure.

Political bodies are mainly concerned with the economy of a country and can be described in terms of the geometric butterfly shape. As already mentioned, the antennae constitute the left and right political economic and social philosophies. Further consideration reveals the four Wings as labour, resources, production and finance hinged to the body, which mixes up consumption and rejection. In the consumer society the Wing of resources is shrinking, the labour Wing is also shrinking due to the expansion of the many and varied instruments of production displacing labour, whereas the financial Wing is expanding, and consumption and rejection have no boundary or classification. In spite of these problems, the sole object is economic growth. Money needs to be injected into the organs at all costs and the spirit which originally sparked the labour force is completely diluted. The fact that man replaced part of his triangular shape with other shapes when at work to enable him to obtain other triangles in exchange for the fulfilment of his spiritual and physical self, was not taken into consideration. Only the final physical output matters and the spirit which guided him is non-existent in economic matters, geared solely at profit making and marketing efficiency etc. When money is exchanged the spirit does not enter the rate of exchange and, because the spirit has not been allocated any space, it cannot be moulded together with the final money output. Neither real fusion nor union exists.

When money is given, the circle of spirit which originally created it has been shattered into pieces. Even if barter replaced money, the actual goods would be considered as physical entities and consideration would not be given to the spirit which created the flower, petrol or any other item or product offered in exchange. The spiritual vacuum constitutes a void which nobody in the financial world thinks of filling up so that there's no sun replacement of the spirit at all. G-d has been replaced by other gods, but money has not been basically replaced. If one goes to the stock exchange, one can experience the agitation caused by fluctuations in the market prices of shares, which can enhance the value of a company or downgrade its financial credibility. Such an agitation does not seem to existing places where the spirit is supposed to predominate. Agitation, if it occurs, is usually mainly mechanical through rituals that have overridden the very purpose of spiritual fire.

There has been a voluntary division of religion and politics which has led to a final voluntary division between the spiritual and the physical elements of man, so that the overall pattern at all levels is the emphasis of the importance of man being bound to earth rather than to heaven. Even a work of art that originally springs from the spirit has taken the shape of a value which can be marketed as a tin of processed peas. At universities research is only allowed to expand as long as it concentrates on efficiency. Everything has become finite, including imagination and poetry which have to fit into the political, economical and social system of a nation in order to appeal and sell. The hinge of the butterfly shape associated to the economic structure portrays consumption and rejection as having one body without definition, due to the standardization of production that has occurred both in instruments of consumption and in the human element. This rejection of individualism has led to spiritual self-denial. This spiralling consumption and rejection lack spirit or reason, except for the ultimate production of wealth, and in this mad pursuit, take no cognizance of individual needs or requirements either physically or spiritually. Non-conformity is considered a renegade act or an interference in the planned exploitation of man by forcing him to comply with the consumer society's impulse of increasing consumption by rejection at an alarming rate, ignoring those natural provisions governing consumption and rejection according to which the physical must be balanced with the spiritual for man or nations to fly within their own structure.

The whole structure of politics and economics is malfunctioning because it is geared to influencing the human kind who has not found its structure, so we always come back to this basic problem. If man had found his own structure which was gearing towards perfection, he would not give high importance to politics and economics since he would be a natural politician and economist. For his decisions, he would not need a superficially concentrated pole to direct his action, but eventually some kind of direction could be given to him when necessary, within some appointed member of his community rather than from a nameless and faceless authoritarian organization external to his way of life. For this to be applied man has to know himself, through the meaning of the daily movement of his Wings which have developed into gestures and through full awareness of geometrical language. From this awareness he could solve most of his problems, ailments and, by learning how to use his own resources, he would find his real purpose and teach institutions to reconsider basic human normal behaviour, such as talking to a neighbour, members of his family instead of resorting consistently to psychiatrists and drugs as a problem occurs. With his newly found vision he would at last understand that by consuming and consuming without rejecting, he would take the risk of producing an outgrowth in all or some elements of his structure and finally break his harmonious balance. His constant aim should be at reshaping his structure, element by element, to allow movement both at his physical and spiritual level. All his purpose would be concentrated on putting some order into his feathers, so that they may work efficiently and stop hindering his flight. Only at this stage will he be able to communicate with others, achieving understanding, not only through speech, but through body language, graffiti, sound and figure language. Once this second stage is achieved, a real mixture can be genuinely concocted and blended together to enable him to perfect his structure allowing him to become an individual free to express himself with help of other individuals and so obtain that perfect balance of spiritual and physical awareness, which is his birthright and was the intention of his Creator in the beginning.

Chapter XVII
Relationships

Relationships are also based on the physical and the moral aspects. To fully understand all the intricacies of how people affect each other, it is necessary to give some background to this highly applicable subject. First, it would appear that in nature an animal and a plant thrive when there are others of its own kind in its surroundings. For example, the willow tree thrives far better if it is in a cluster of willow trees; the same applies to animals. This illustrates, that even in nature, without our mode of communication and no matter how basic or primitive the living object may be, it will not thrive so well as a single entity. To analyze this even further it is necessary to reduce this aspect of nature to movement, consumption, rejection, expansion and contraction. When a whole diversity of consumption is introduced into the structure it leads to a movement of concentration, followed by contraction. Then when it is fully processed, the waste product is ejected out of the system leaving the usable product to expand within the structure. This represents the main overall movement, but there exists two basic and different alternatives both at the physical and moral level. Dealing with the physical aspect first, there is the case of consumption not being properly classified before introduction into the structure so there cannot exist full contraction or expansion and some of the useful product is dissipated in the waste, conversely some of the waste is not rejected and is caught up in the useful product which is undergoing expansion. Then there is the case of consumption not being classified at all. This results in rejection taking place at both ends of the structure, without taking into consideration that which belongs to the spiritual.

Concerning the moral aspect, it is necessary to maintain the same system of analysis. Therefore, when a whole diversity of moral input is introduced into the mental structure, it leads to a movement of concentration followed by contraction. Then when it is fully absorbed, the unusable material is rejected upwards leaving that which is of value to expand within the mental process. This represents the main overall movement. However, there exist two basic and different alternatives. The case where moral input is not properly classified before introduction into the moral structure so that there cannot exist full contraction or expansion and some of the useful material is dissipated in the rejection process and conversely some of this rejection is caught up into the useful material which is undergoing expansion. Then there is the case of consumption not being classified at all and this results in rejection taking place downwards.

It will be seen from the above that there are many possibilities when mixing one particular physical pattern to one particular moral pattern. For instance, a man who has not correctly classified consumption might try to relate to another man or woman who has not classified moral input at all or, as another example, a woman who has correctly classified the moral material might not have classified at all physical consumption. Since the gap becomes even wider when the source of moral intake varies, there exist almost countless possibilities of relationships and each pattern may display smoother or sharper angles at particular levels. This has created the diversity of relationships between man and man, woman and woman, man and woman. Of course, the ideal relationship occurs when consumption is correctly classified in the physical sense as well as in the moral aspect. In other words, when moral movements are based on a philosophy rating mutual respect as one of the top priorities. Unfortunately, this is rarely the case because in all three relationships – man to woman, man to man, woman to woman – the attraction is to shapes, regardless of their movements, which they do not recognize. The above has been related to the human being because he is basically a cultural animal, with the ability of choice through reason, rather than sole instinct.

In order to understand ourselves within the human structure at its present stage of varied development, it is essential to try and visualize what might have been our pre-earthly life. This can still be foreseen through the voidless law of nature ruled by a movement of ceaseless expansion and concentration. At pre-earth level we may have been solely souls accumulating knowledge through a concentration of light.

This light may have been the Torah passed on to man by G-d as a guide to enable him to create harmonious relationships. This passing of knowledge seems to have been primarily visual and supported by pulsations, so that it could be mostly forgotten once entering the earth level in order to be re-learned through experiences. After this concentration of light, expansion followed for the soul to be ready to descend on to earth. The same movement occurred as the child within the womb concentrated all his physical energies to receive his soul and it would take him a lifetime to expand his built-in dissipated light of knowledge.

There is no clock timing as far as the soul entering the structure is concerned. The period of time is dependent upon the necessary pulsations required before becoming ready. So, there is a whole process of learning, dissipating knowledge and relearning before an individual develops the antennae that will guide him through the philosophy that he has taken a great part in creating himself with his own hands while a doctor listens to the heart beat of a baby still in the womb counting the number of heart beats. The baby himself while being contained within his mother's structure is being shaped through her heart beat, the vibrations of her voice and other sounds surrounding her, as well as through her general movement, both of locomotion and body language. Once the baby enters the world, the sound of language is extended through visual language which takes the shape of light, but at a far-less concentrated level. The element of feeling and touch is also added to communication, while the soul was deprived of this element since it was not yet contained in a dense physical structure. From this analysis one question is predominating: why is there so much emphasis in articulated speech for communication once we are adults when such a close communication allowed closely knit relationships without it at the early stage of development? The answer may be that we have allowed "articulated" speech to expand at the expense of communication through movement of a geometrical shape. Yet a most modern research in linguistics, whose enterprise is to communicate to a computer as much understanding as possible about human language, resorts to geometrical patterns in order to fulfil this purpose at the computer programming level. In this particular effort, the computer is being fed with triangles, squares and circles grooved on bowls and the correct plug has to be fitted into the correct groove following the meaning of the sentence and a code according to which a triangular shape might be associated to an animate, the square shape to an inanimate, etc.

The lack of harmonious relationships that can be witnessed today, which has led to a fragmented society, has been mainly due to a lack of understanding of the second type of communication. Following the theory of movement, the problem seems mainly due to mistiming. If person "A" is in process of expansion while person "B" tries to force that person to experience more concentration, the movement does not fit and type two communication breaks down. As an example, if person "A" has just read a book, has completed the concentration movement and is in the process of assimilating it, performing an expansion movement while "B" either a person or mass media pushes another book down his throat, thus requiring concentration instead of expansion from him, genuine dialogue is impossible.

There are many examples in daily life that show that the person is not ready to concentrate or expand, but the rhythm of life goes beyond the movement of the individual and his body shape seems to fit in while his spirit is miles apart. Serious deterioration may occur when even his spirit has to follow the general movement and is thus being annihilated through a lack of coordination to such an extent, that his initial movement has been destroyed and forgotten and he is being replaced by a movement which is external to his structure. How can communication improve? Simply by making the effort of understanding one's own movement and pace it to the movement of others, so that some unity of rhythm can be obtained. This can be further explained through silent observation of body language. As an example, straight after reading a book or watching a film, a person may stretch his or her arms outwards in a relaxing movement. The idea is not to stop this movement which takes place and to wait until it has fully stopped before introducing another element which should require contraction rather than more expansion.

The movement might be disconnected and diverted and may lose its full meaning and any philosophy which may enter the structure at any time, such as commercialism which, while being forced into our mental structure, deadens the true spirit of man, preventing him from listening to his own movement as well as to those of others and preventing him from acting in the correct direction. There is an old language, the understanding of which we have forgotten, that is so elaborate in its simplicity that it cannot be communicated to a computer. It relates back to emotions expressed by a particular movement of energies, displayed both in facial and bodily expressions, with concentration mainly through stoppage of reflection, letting loose physical emotions such as anger, fear, passion, jealousy etc.

These emotions divert the essential energies leading to the basic movement referred to above and, for this purpose, let us return to the butterfly shape. The top Wings represent the moral and spiritual, the bottom Wings the physical hinged to the body which is either divided or unified, the antennae being that which attract the emotions. If the attraction causes the wrong emotional reactions, unclassified consumption is formed, bringing about an imbalance of consumption and rejection, so causing the lower physical Wings to become stronger and the top spiritual Wings to become weaker with the result that the structure becomes dismantled and shapeless.

It is this constant uneven movement in its many varied forms that created the problems and difficulties in relationships as they reflect and deflect energies that are weakening and dismantling rather than balancing the structure between one human and another.

So far, we have considered shape only in a geometrical sense without instilling movement. We have also considered movement without containing it into a shape so that we have separated sound language from visual language. Now, when the two elements of shape and movement are connected, life appears and the butterfly, which is man, can fly.

There is nothing more emotional than seeing a butterfly emerge from its chrysalis and take its first three-dimensional flight to freedom.

It is strange to note that when taking such a flight we are not even conscious of its direction as we have become totally unaware of the significance of the points of the compass, i.e., east, west, south and north. Most of us are blissfully unaware of the direction we are facing at any particular moment and, if asked, would probably say north when we are facing east.

It is doubtful whether we even know in what direction we face when sleeping. This, plus the fact that few of us can read time from the stars or the position of the sun, is a dimension which has gradually become lost by us. In this way we have cut our relationship and link with nature.

Relationship is basically three-dimensional and can be analysed as the interaction between oneself, G-d, and others. The whole relationship can only stand providing it has a full growth and understanding of one's movement and shape. Once this movement and shape is fully understood, one can concentrate towards absolute direct communication with our Maker without the need of intermediaries who have the effect of diluting our relationship with G-d. After this relationship comes the communication with others, a relationship that does not distract from one's own movement and purpose so long as moderation prevails.

To fully understand the process of relationships, the body of Aleph, the first letter of the Hebrew alphabet, can again be utilized for analytical purposes. As we said, the Aleph can be described as two yods, which have the appearance of commas, on each side of a linked wand. One comma with its head up represents the spiritual aspect, the other with its head down represents the physical aspect, the wand being that which receives both the spiritual and the physical input and output. If the commas are described as the Wings both top and bottom united into one, each Wing must move in unison with the other to obtain a balanced flight within the body and hinge.

The ideal relationship between man and woman occurs when their shapes and movement correspond in every detail so that when man enters woman they're fused into an Aleph and become one. This then means that they are moving as one entity in one direction. However, it is often the case that the shape and movement of the man does not correspond to that of the woman or vice versa. The reason for this is that either woman or man or both have not been able to fuse their Wings together and, instead, each set of Wings have become imperfectly linked so that since the same movement and shape cannot take place, there will ultimately arrive a point in time when a cleavage will take place as there is no possibility of becoming one and moving in the same direction. When this occurs, man and woman become two and cease to think and fly three dimensionally and instead think in four dimensions. It being already difficult to operate in three dimensions, adding a fourth makes it virtually impossible for such a relationship to last and it is destined to eventually contract and fragment.

This is emphasized when considering relationships with others. There is the ideal position where the Aleph is obtained so that there is unity between man and woman (Yod 1) and unity between all the others (Yod 2) and both Yods being hinged together through the wand of G-d allowing the whole system to be unified. The second alternative is that Yod 1 is broken into two when man and woman cannot obtain unity or when oneself cannot obtain unity, whereas Yod 2 has obtained unity. In this situation there is still four-dimensional thinking, even if it occurs because of one or two individuals. The third situation is when Yod 1 is not united and most of the elements of Yod 2 are not united so that there is multi-dimensional thinking leading to multi-fragmentation in spite of G-d's wand still maintaining some kind of order in between these poles.

Within this analysis one realizes the importance of education in shaping the spirit and movement of individuals. Ideally, education is at its best when it allows a return to the original shape and movement fitted with built-in basic guiding principles. When driving a car one should check the speedometer in order not to go too fast and keep control of the vehicle. The same applies in the process of relationships when it is advisable not to go too fast in order to maintain thought in three dimensions. When one follows this discipline, one adapts to the routine of checking all the time, maintaining a balance in order not to lose one's original entity. This movement is not as easy as the one which dictates us to pick up ready-made products from shelves and throw them away, but it is worthwhile in the long run. The second movement, which is based on expansion, will lead to contraction as opposed to the movement starting with contraction and ending up in a full expansion which is the basis of the philosophy put forward in this book. When educating a child, parents should take into account the original shape and movement of their children and check that both are preserved and not destroyed. By so doing they give full texture to the basic purpose and meaning of life and mutual respect will be achieved.

The same basic premise can be applied to education as a whole, for example, enough care not to tread on the other's Wing.

There is also in relationships those who are lonely. This is due to people who are unable to fuse their Wings together in one unified movement so that separation occurs with the individual and is projected towards the others because the concept of G-d has been bypassed. It is as if man forgot that he originated from a chrysalis which had internal spiritual movement that came into shape and fuller movement when the butterfly came in to being. So, instead of expanding both his spiritual and physical energies into the others, all the energies are retracted and finally dissipated.

There are basically two types of people. First, those who have remained in the spiritual chrysalis and have refused to move away from it. Therefore, their Wings become fused and prevent movement. This restricts the development of the soul into a still shape, and thus does not take into account the fact that originally the spiritual force was designed for its movement to be contained in a shape that could give more texture and weight to the spirit born in a finite shape. By destroying that finite shape and giving it an infinite dimension peculiar to G-d alone, one is destroying the very purpose of our Maker and by doing so damages his dimension.

The second type is the one that concentrates solely on the shape and disregards the original chrysalis as part of his evolution. Thus, the first is without body and shape and the second, in spite of some kind of external movement, has no antennae that give the movement its full meaning. The second type relegates G-d's creation of man to that of animals by killing the spirit and over emphasising the importance of the shape, thus also damaging another dimension of G-d. There are obviously many subtle variations between these two extreme poles which do not achieve fulfilment in either way. People entering these two main categories damage either their shape or movement and by so doing, damage that of others when a relationship occurs, leading to disintegration in the overall movement and shape.

Even if only one person enters either of these categories, damage can be unlimited and the whole shape and movement of the overall relationship can lead to a total deterioration and ruin harmony on an extensive scale, so that the balanced Aleph becomes fragmented between the unifying wand, which loses most of its power or fusion.

This is particularly relevant to the body politic and the mass media, who concentrate their efforts on the population as a whole without consideration being given to the individual and how their actions damage the shape and movement of individuals within society. Referring to the basic shape of oneself, G-d and others, it would be true to say that government and the body politic tend to bypass G-d and over emphasize oneself and others at the expense of the coordinated triangle of three elements. They make G-d into a political football or a piece of clay which, they try to mould to their own will.

This also applies to religion in that it has been channelled to become an instrument taking advantage of individuals

Relationships

who have sought its help for communication purposes. In religions, official intermediaries have become, through rigid theory, dogma and ritual, counter-productive. This has in fact created a blockage which has broken the triangle and distorted it into a two-dimensional movement. The Wings are still flapping but the contracting and expanding movement has ceased to function. This has, in the main, created a void leaving many still seeking a way of direct communication with G-d. Many have to resort to a medley assortment of negative and highly damaging sects which have developed due to the lack of movement by the official representatives of the G-dly spirit. This breakdown has occurred in both cases because the individual has failed to recognize the possibilities of his own resources.

The truth of the matter is that man no longer thinks in three dimensions but only in two. This is entirely due to his obsession with his physical being and his desire for quick expansion at the expense of contraction. He wants consumption without restriction and the ability to reject at will. He is unconcerned with respecting the shape or movement of nature of conscious reproduction. To assist him in his physical obsession he will create many sophisticated two-dimensional instruments regardless of the consequences that will force him to retract drastically. The third dimension imposes restrictions before expansion and this is intolerable to his development within the consumer society where consumption has a higher rating than the concept of G-d and where there is no room for the basic triangle to expand in its natural movement. Therefore, relationships are not deeply linked or coordinated as communication becomes increasingly stifled by the distortion of shape and movement until a situation is created where there exists nothing to replace the basic triangle of life.

Although there are those who revert to the basic triangle and create adaptations to the three-dimensional thinking, they are not recognized during their own lifetime. Instead, they are swallowed up in the rapidly expanding structure of the masses who adorn the physical aspects of life. Other generations might give them more time and their wisdom might be understood. Thus, there is no hope that change will occur and that man may adopt the "new" facet of the triangle of life, which is part of the equation that is to be solved and complied with.

A stand could be made in order to achieve this equation by listening to the movement of children who have not been spoiled by political and religious translators. By doing so, we can renew and give a new lease of life to our movement which can then be directed towards both primitive and sophisticated instructions. In this way we will concentrate on developing human sciences in conjunction with exact sciences thereby causing the young generation to begin thinking in a three-dimensional manner and, therefore, to start to create solid relationships.

Chapter XVIII
SHAPE, MOVEMENT AND WINGS

The multiple movements allotted to human beings are ultimately produced by his Wings, the shape of which does not appear as clearly as in birds. The vision is deceitful: the Wings of birds appear as two mere triangles but, with closer observation, one can notice that each Wing is in fact composed of two triangles, linked up at a slight angle to allow a sophisticated movement that appears to be reduced to flight. Ocular witnesses are not the Court's favourites.

Birds when flying together do not seem to fly in one particular direction or purpose in their daily activities. However, when a climactic situation occurs such as at the time of migration to another warmer land where they will temporarily settle their abode, they all assemble in their flight to form an overall triangle, the triangle of migratory birds.

Although we are not aware of it in our daily actions, we project our spirit though our shape, movement and Wings, and our unawareness is solely due to the perfect level of our physical performance. The "problem" is that our metaphysical side is still to be moulded by ourselves. It does not work in an efficient automatic manner as its physical counterpart. It needs to be shaped by us through the controlled movement of our Wings performing actions. It is difficult to find a human example which can be compared to that of the pattern of migratory birds, except perhaps during the deployment of various military forces at military parades, although they appear far more hollow in their purpose than those of birds geared by the instinct of survival.

We also seem to be fitted with two basic triangles within our Wings as with birds, our legs and arms working as one, our second triangle being given to us by our hands and fingers which form another Wing and our Wings within a Wing, which can project multiple instruments of Wings distracting further and further our instinct of survival. A chair is no more a chair to sit on, but a twelfth century antique to be looked at through a museum window. Our shape would have no life unless it had a movement. The same applies to movement that would have no effect unless it was contained within an active shape. Both movement and shape are projected through Wings which show that, even at our physical level, we are activated in three dimensions. The texture of life can be seen and felt through shape, it can be felt and heard through movement and generally assessed through shape and movement of Wings. It is impossible to define one without linking it to the other two aspects. This is part of the overall pattern of life which leaves no room for a void and links everything to give life a deeper character. If one element is missing, man is handicapped unless he can fill this void. There are many recognized handicapped people surrounding us and the welfare government gives them some help to fill their own void as much as possible. But some of the most handicapped people are ourselves. Although we have these three elements, we fail to coordinate them because we concentrate on one aspect and ignore the other two.

It would seem that man can change or manipulate his shape, movement and Wings separately or in a combined action. As far as shape is concerned, a man can, through selection and conception, change his shape through his offspring by selecting a particular mate and not another, so he has some choice before conception. This selection seems to apply to Darwin's theory of evolution, but, while in the animal world only useful characteristics that are kept, in the human world there does not appear to be such a classification. The concept of beauty prevails over that of usefulness.

Human beings have also tried to change their shape after conception, again through their idea of beauty according to the outlook of harmonious shape in their culture. For instance, small feet in Chinese women, longnecks and ear lobes in some African tribes.

Alteration also occurs by means of transforming movement through consumption. We have mentioned previously the effect of pills. There is also the effect of daily food products. This latter consumption seems to have stimulated man's imagination. See, for example, Popeye who is stronger after swallowing some spinach, as if a miracle solution to our weaknesses could be achieved merely through a chemical process. The consumption of new ideas and philosophies has produced far more reaching changes in man's movement, as in Freudian theory and Marxist philosophy, which demonstrate that a metaphysical solution can be far more influential than a chemical one in the long run. This is the difference between cocaine and ideology.

The third alteration can be applied to the Wings and, in particular, to our gestures which have varied through time, mainly through change of habits, environment and the creation of instruments. It seems that a Wing lost is replaced by another. When we walk bare-footed, our feet arch into quite a high angle, but when we wear shoes, the angle is restricted. This is particularly so with high heeled shoes worn by women. They hardly form an angle when the women walk, but, on the other hand, they appeal to men and, therefore, achieve the Wing of attraction. This is a transformation of the Wing of locomotion for a different purpose.

The fact is that, although the shape of man and the Wing is of vital importance to him, neither of these elements have any significant value without movement. It is in the way a man moves that he is able not only to change his destiny or radically alter his way of life in all its aspects, but also govern the shape of his Wings. It is this ability to select certain movements that distinguishes man from other living entities. Also important is the way he flaps or moves his Wings. The extent and direction of movement will determine not only his physical and spiritual structure, but what he consumes and rejects, what success and failure he will obtain, what life style he will aspire to and what work he will carry out. Lack of movement will cause the shape of the Wings to contract, whereas more movement will cause it to expand. This in itself will either create atrophy or energetic use in man. The problem for man is to correctly balance shape, Wing and movement so that his spirit and his physical being achieve perfect harmony and enable him to maintain an even performance throughout the varying cycles of his life.

Basically, man has not changed in his shape since his original creation. The main change has been concerned with his movement which has altered the impact of his Wings towards both the physical and spiritual aspects. We have seen how far the development of instruments and sophisticated apparatus was to some extent responsible for this and made him addicted to his physical being, leaving less and less room for his spiritual movement to expand.

This situation has directed his movement away from survival so that man is becoming less and less able to control either himself or the environment in which he lives. Therefore, he no longer occupies the position, which was originally given to him, for example, to expand the eternal creative Wing of G-d, but has moved his Wing and shape in a disconnected direction.

Man is unknowingly endeavouring to discard his Wings and to rely totally on his hinge of consumption and rejection in a consumer society, which, although giving the impression of shape and movement, is shapeless and exists in a purposeless void where positive movement towards eternity has almost become extinct. Even the movement of picking up a book from the shelves of a book-shop resembles the picking up of items in a supermarket.

Man seems to have replaced his spirit with physical expediency in that he produces instruments that no longer have the inner spirit involved in the construction. Mass production on the conveyor belt system in factories has evolved with the result that the finished object is completely void of spirit and hence of life. For example, the glut of books and ideas corresponds to the glut of consumable products, illustrating that lack of genuine spiritual movement, even in the reading of books, has reached even man's movements at work.

Even in the beginning, man, when working, was giving up part of his three-dimensional entity. A cabinet maker was imprinting part of his spirit into the piece of furniture he was creating both from new wood and from his coordinated movement with a hammer and saw. The cabinet maker in the twentieth century in a factory does not project the three-dimensional man. Instead, several men touched the wood with shapeless Wings and produced the final output without extra dimension. Devaluation of work, and man giving away part of his creative triangle, is another phenomenon displaying a spiritual void. This devaluation in work will reproduce a shunting effect at all levels that will have some repercussions at communication, love and religious levels, and produce more and more divorces both within man himself and with the world surrounding him. Divorce is in a way a symptom displaying openly the rejection of shapeless movements and appears to some as freedom, i.e., more movement within the shape. Yet shaped movement is being suppressed even outside psychiatric hospitals, but in a far more subtle way by voluntary diversions instead of pills, injections or electric shocks. It is a miracle how man still survives in spite of this lack of genuine movement, suppressed not only from within, but also from external rules and statutes that increase stillness. It is a surprise that some men continue to move in spite of all the compelling forces that obstruct his articulated movement. Perhaps this remnant of movement is due to some extinct dissidents who resist the effect of the sausage machine and manage, in spite of the media and ourselves, to convey the message of our basic needs and longings.

If the hammer and saw function together by coordinating a vertical and horizontal movement, some coordination can also be expected from some of our mental tools such as comedy, diplomacy or fear, for us to revert into ourselves and even regress in order to move forward at a later stage.

The different paths taken to achieve this creative regression do not matter as long as the end result – achieving genuine movement – is obtained. Whether it be through Buddhism, Marxism, right or left ideology or science is of no crucial importance as long as the other final output is true communication.

Man has been blinded to the reality that surrounds him whilst the multiplicity of signs exists at all times before his eyes. He either refuses to accept that they exist or is ignorant of their meaning or existence. However, the spiritual and physical triangle is imprinted within his core; it cannot be eliminated since it also contains the spark, which enables him to find life worthwhile regardless of his efforts to follow a current external to his own path.

Perhaps the physical survival of man is due to the print of the three-dimensional triangle within the anatomy of his instinct. This triangle that he can unconsciously visualize throughout his life gives him this necessary inborn balance which has enabled him to live on in spite of some of his shapeless and motionless Wings.

Chapter XIX
THE PSYCHOLOGY OF THE TRIANGULAR PHILOSOPHY

When G-d conceived man in his imagination as a physical entity, He saw him like angels with Wings enabling him free flight both physically and spiritually. Yet these were invisible to man in his earthly creation and, although they existed, he was unable to see them except through some inspired paintings portraying archangels with Wings. Only when he has achieved some degree of perfection through many cycles of life and experience will he be able to glimpse the beautiful outline of his being fitted with Wings that he does not feel as an essential part of his being. They will then allow his soul free flight upwards to his Maker on the return journey. The Wings existed on his original downward flight to physical life but, once he had landed, the Wings were no longer visible to him and he lost their feel and touch. From that moment on, his sole destiny in life was to rediscover his true self and be aware of the existence of the spiritual Wings that will allow him to return from whence he came.

Countless artists, sculptors, writers have portrayed man with Wings and many triangles. Is this just coincidence or does this inspiration originate from his soul to convey into him a momentary glimpse of the vision that he is and can be?

Man knows of the existence of the triangle which exists in every phase and aspect of his life but, he has lost the ability to recognize its vital importance to his own self. Woman came from his triangle (rib) and because of this she too has Wings in the same way as man. By containing man's Wing, she has become the recipient of life.

What then is the psychology behind the triangle? It seems to be based on Pythagoras's theorem, that is, in any right-angled triangle the square of the hypotenuse is equal to the sum of the squares on the other two sides. When searching for a right-angled triangle in the human face, the most prominent one is that which starts at the bridge of the nose descends to the nostrils, then goes to the hole in the ear. In this triangle the square on the hypotenuse comprises that area which goes from the bridge of the nose to the ear and then incorporates half of the area of the head. The other two squares are, the one which is from the nostrils to the ear, then that area which includes the lower part of the cheek, jaw and chin. The other square is that which lies from the bridge of the nose down to the nostrils and incorporates the higher cheek and jaw bones.

It would appear that in the human, the right-angled triangle is composed of sight, smell and hearing, the square on the hypotenuse is that which incorporates the brain and controls linguistics which is equal to the sum of the squares on the other two sides which permits of articulation, consumption and rejection.

The right-angled triangle is that which incorporates everything in man's survival and – above all through his sight, hearing and smell – dictates his thoughts and actions. Further, the eyes mirror his soul and are the apex of his three-dimensional self. Without this triangle man could not exist as this is the spiral of life, the very theorem of his existence. Everything else stems from this triangle of life including reproduction and the shape and movement of his Wings and the instruments which he creates. Also incorporated in man's face are six further triangles, six being the multiple of the original three which is unity through the triangle and represents his three-dimensional self. The two main triangles being from the bridge of the nose to the hole in the ear then to the mouth at each side of the face, yet they appear as one from the two ear holes to the point of the chin, but in fact this triangle is composed of the two mentioned above. It therefore appears, like the Wing of a bird, made out of one triangle but is in fact composed out of two, to allow a multi-directional movement, similar to the possible movements that go from our thumb to our fingers, from our legs to our thighs, from our forearms to our biceps, then from our hands to our arms and from our feet to our legs. Also, from the higher to the lower part of our body.

It would seem that everything is as one, yet it is in fact two opposing forces and each part of the opposing forces is incorporated to the other through a common channel, as with the two small circles of the Tao symbol which include the opposing forces of the YIN and YANG.

In the same way as the human triangle, the three-dimensional aspect seems to be imprinted in man's tissular memory at the level of all man's senses of perception. For example, in the Highway Code the triangle signifies danger and in the Catholic ritual there is the triangular movement from head to chest. This is also extended by the words in the name of three entities. Women naturally plait their hair in three separate strands and some of them do a three plait bread for unknown conscious reasons.

Generally, a date is defined by three figures representing a specific day, month and year. One may wonder why three numbers are required and why the triangle has been selected at all levels. The explanation may lie in the fact that the circle can be easily integrated and absorbed into our brain as a natural process because it does not have any sharp angles that draw concentration. Other shapes such as squares, hexagons, pentagons have so many sides and angles that they lead to distractions of the brain and do not appeal to concentration. So it seems that the triangle and the figure three appeal to the mind as the vital hinge, which will produce concentration and unity, and avoid unnoticed absorption or distraction leading to fragmentation. The figure three will represent the sufficient number of poles geared towards our spiritual and physical survival. For the ancient Egyptians, whether the base of a pyramid was square of polygonal did not alter the fact that the final massive stone structure had its sloping sides meeting at an apex and forming triangles. The apex, the point of concentration of the structure, was reflected through the triangular shape in climactic holy performances such as the building of a royal tomb for the ancient Egyptians and the pyramid as platform for sanctuaries of the Mayas. It is also significant that the Christian cross which focuses into the meeting point projects four triangles. Similarly, most other religious symbols that exist can be basically reduced down to the triangular shape, containing the spiritual structure. Even the Cabbalistic tree of man is linked up through triangles. Any other additional aspects only build up around the triangle and the figure three. They are only supplementary elements which may distract from the original concept of the triangle. If a triangle lets another additional figure enter its structure it will no longer be a triangle, but another geometrical shape can be divided into triangles until the original triangle will appear to the mind so that the movement is one of expansion and contraction. Further, the vital movement of expansion and contraction can only be contained within the triangle so that it does not seem to be chance that the embryo of life grows and develops within woman's triangular pelvis, the culminating output of which is a triangular pain when the baby has left the triangle of his mother and consumes his food from her figure three.

So basically, within our daily existence it seems that we act without reason, but in fact it appears that we act within the reason of our tissular memory, which responds and is guided by the psychology of the triangular philosophy.

The nose (nostrils) is the organ into which G-d breathed

life into man and it would seem that it is the apex of all the triangles that come from the circular base of the skull. Further, even the heart beat is graphically depicted as a series of peaks and valleys which give the appearance of open-ended triangles which cease to exist at death, when the breath of life ceases.

Therefore, the triangle is the sign that man so diligently seeks as proof of the living G-d. Yet man fails to recognize that in every aspect of his being and environment the sign is plainly visible. Like a spider he weaves his web in blindness and stumbles in the darkness of his ignorance, either because in his tissular memory there exists a desire to challenge G-d or because he has failed to link up his hinge with his Wings. Hence his flight, which is erratic and purposeless and his failure to reach the apex of unity are caused by his creation of many apexes that both confuse and distract him from achieving in practice a perfect structure.

Chapter XX
The Spiritual and Physical Linkage

Architecture projects a message beyond time as does any genuine work of art. Every meaningful action is done by and interrelated to the spirit. Without it the gesture only comes from the flesh and is purely mechanical. This spirit wanes out and so does the flesh as a secondary effect. This can be understood by referring to the story of Aladdin and his lamp; a genie came out from it and was given the possibility to express its potential and work in conjunction with the physical structure of Aladdin instead of being a mere gadget. This applies to any man who leaves some outlet for his spirit.

This story and many others show how the spirit is linked to the physical structure and how it is well set in its position only if man is comfortable in his flesh. In the same way the mystical experience of religion basically corresponds to scientific data as shown by Newton who only revealed his mathematical findings once he had clearly established spiritually that they corresponded to the "hidden" religious knowledge. Parallel to the correlation between flesh and spirit there is a link between science and religion. This experience of Newton has been exhibited by most great scientists as can be judged by a study of the lives of Einstein, Darwin etc. Science without religion is flesh without spirit and religion without science is spirit without flesh. In linguistics the same applies between the bodily shape of words and their actual

Chapter XX The Spiritual and Physical Linkage

meaning. If this link is not recognized then nature becomes either purely scientific or purely poetic. It has recently been discovered that the two hemispheres in the human cortex dealing with imagination and with reasoning are connected so that there is no dichotomy in a man being engrossed in both scientific and theological research.

The reason for some forms of act being more successful at one period of time than another is linked to the situation existing within man's spirit and physical structure. It is not unusual for painters with genius to be fully appreciated only by following generations. The spirit of man is usually one step ahead of its physical vehicle.

There is no chance either in the existence of the twelve tribes. We have four basic Wings which overall have twelve sides, each side having a particular purpose in life that can bring an overall movement brought forward through a connection and interrelation. The thirteenth tribe is made out of the members of the twelve tribes that did not fit the main structure and thereby disorientated the main purpose of each tribe or unbalanced their Wings. As in the flight of birds there will be no genuine balance and power until these misfits can find their appropriate space within their original tribe so that the pectoral atrophied muscles that control their own Wing can be put back into full use again. Until then they will remain as seeds that will propagate the false Torah and its devilish face that hurts and scars humanity.

Even so, man in the ancient past depicted himself as having apart animal and part human body, thus displaying his desire that he should retain his identity and Wings no matter with what devilish physical force lets himself assailed with. Examples of this are Pegasus, the centaur, griffin and sphinx.

The human aspect is preserved from head to waist displaying a longing to preserve the spiritual part of man and a need to protect the human Wing from its animal counterpart.

In birds the pectoral muscles that allow them brilliance

and power in the air through the instrument of their Wings are heavier than the rest of the muscular mass. In man the same pectoral muscles only weigh one seventeenth of the rest of his muscles. While the whole skeleton of birds is adapted to their Wings, man's skeleton is not. Perhaps man's spirit has been added to the human structure to counteract this together with the instrument of man's hand in which all the fingers, with the exception of the thumb, are composed of three phalanges hence consisting in a Wing in its own right that allows the bi-phalanged thumb to obtain its third dimension when in its contact.

It may be because of this blatant lack of muscular support that our Wings have weakened but the major explanation seems to lie in the under-rating of the spiritual potential that enables man to reach his own particular flight. Our fear of losing balanced power of our Wings appears in various symptoms such as mythology, divorces, fragmentation of our society and a lack of mutual trust down to cancer.

The triangular shape of our hip bones being larger than the triangular bones of our shoulder blades is not simply due to fulfil the physical need of our legs carrying more weight. Our hands, legs, face and our whole body in fact also carry a large part of our spiritual weight through our daily actions and, as if the sign was not obvious enough, our face is inundated with triangles to physically channel our actions by relating them into our spirit.

The point is that, the more we endeavour to suppress our spiritual links, the more they reappear, because the spirit irradiates and, in the last analysis, it can neither be burned by fire nor destroyed by water or polluted by air. It is written under our tongue and in the triangular shape of the pain of life at the precious moment of a baby sucking his mother and emphasizing the triangle of her womb.

It is written in all aspects of life and in the geographical map of our earth. England is a small triangle pointing upwards, an independent island which has produced so many

Chapter XX The Spiritual and Physical Linkage

philosophers. France, on the other hand, has hexagonal shape which produced a Cartesian spirit often lacking imagination. Under France, there is the Italian boot kicking all this towards the very earthly Russian empire. This Russian paganism is in its turn counterbalanced as with a plumb-line by the animism of the Chinese continent. On the other side and through the hinge of the small crescent of Palestine, there is the African continent diametrically opposed to this mass. By its humanism largely fitting its triangular shape pointing downwards, it counterbalances the effects provoked by the European Industrial Revolution. The same analysis applies to North America counterbalanced by South America.

Our world and our body well enough appear to be regulated as the mechanism of a clock. Can our spirit fit or will it eternally escape the logical language of life?

www.ingramcontent.com/pod-product-compliance
Lightning Source LLC
Chambersburg PA
CBHW070641050426
42451CB00008B/259